on
poverty

Dickens **on** poverty

edited by Pete Orford

'on'

'on'

Published by Hesperus Press Limited
28 Mortimer Street, London W1W 7RD
www.hesperuspress.com

First published by Hesperus Press Limited, 2013

Designed and typeset by Fraser Muggeridge studio
Printed and bound in Great Britain by CPI Group (UK) Ltd

ISBN: 978-1-84391-620-8

Contents

Introduction

> They were a boy and girl. Yellow, meagre, ragged, scowling, wolfish; but prostrate, too, in their humility. Where graceful youth should have filled their features out, and touched them with its freshest tints, a stale and shrivelled hand, like that of age, had pinched, and twisted them, and pulled them into shreds. Where angels might have sat enthroned, devils lurked, and glared out menacing. No change, no degradation, no perversion of humanity, in any grade, through all the mysteries of wonderful creation, has monsters, half so horrible and dread [...]
>
> 'They are Man's' said the spirit, looking down upon them. 'And they cling to me, appealing from their fathers. This boy is Ignorance. This girl is Want. Beware them both, and all of their degree, but most of all beware this boy, for on his brow I see that written which is Doom, unless the writing be erased.'

Scrooge's encounter with Ignorance and Want in *A Christmas Carol* seems peculiar at first, being a moment of allegory in a journey that is otherwise predominately personal to him. But on closer reflection, while these children, who cling so desperately to the Spirit of Christmas Present, are in one sense of universal relevance, as a consequence of that they are, by definition, of personal relevance too: Dickens felt it was every person's responsibility not only to beware Ignorance and Want, but to *be aware* of them. In an age before a state welfare system, before national pensions and social workers, the fate of the poor and destitute was determined by the charity of others. Some chose to ignore this; others, like Dickens, found such a feat impossible. As he writes in 'Wapping Workhouse', he would wander 'in the streets of a city where every stone seemed to call to me, as I walked along, "Turn this way, man, and see what waits to be done!'" Poverty was everywhere he looked, both financial and moral: a lack of money could often lead to a fall in values and ethics, and equally the persistent troubles that blighted the poor could be attributed to the lack of concern and morality in those higher up the social ladder.

It is with this in mind that this selection of Dickens' writings opens with a case that encapsulated everything Dickens was against: the scandal of Bartholomew Drouet and his pauper school in Tooting, where an outbreak of cholera claimed the lives of over 150 children. Drouet himself had kept the children in his school in appalling conditions, barely feeding them and making them sleep four in a bed, even after the outbreak. It was an act such as might be committed by the devilish schoolmaster Squeers in *Nicholas Nickleby*, and yet the Tooting scandal occurred six years after Dickens' novel was written; an unfortunate case of life imitating art. Dickens wrote four pieces for *The Examiner* following the case against Drouet – 'The Paradise at Tooting', 'The Tooting Farm', 'A Recorder's Charge' and 'The Verdict against Drouet' – all of which are included here. The fact that he returned to the topic on four occasions indicates the impact this case made on Dickens, as do the subsequent references to Drouet that may be spotted in later articles in this selection (Alec W. Brice and K.J. Fielding made an in-depth study of Dickens and Drouet in 'Dickens and the Tooting Disaster', *Victorian Studies*, December 1968). In short, Dickens was appalled, not only by the deaths but by the morality of a man who would treat children in such a way. As the case continued, with the shock acquittal of Drouet, his disgust extended from the single figure of Drouet to the entire system that had let this happen, and the realisation that the fortunate should have abandoned and neglected the unfortunate to such a horrifying degree. The case for Drouet argued that he had not taken any action to infect the children with cholera, therefore he could not be held accountable; Dickens felt, quite rightly, that it was the lack of action which made

Drouet guilty, the same lack of action regularly seen throughout the city and which allowed the damage of poverty and deprivation to continue unchecked, later recognised in *Little Dorrit* and its ironic subtitle 'Nobody's fault'.

The articles following this both come from Dickens' early work under the pseudonym of Boz and describe the varying degrees of that poverty which he witnessed first-hand; in 'The Pawnbroker's Shop' (*The Evening Chronicle*, 30 June 1835) and 'Shabby-Genteel People' (*Morning Chronicle*, 5 November 1834), Dickens describes those who are doing what they can to get by, to hold on to both their independence and their dignity. We see here real-life templates of Dickensian characters; the violent man in the pawnbrokers, collecting tools ready for a job of dubious legality, and beating both wife and child, precedes Bill Sikes, Daniel Quilp or Jerry Cruncher, while the shabby-genteel man who tries (unsuccessfully) to disguise his financial woes with an air of gentility foreshadows Mr Micawber and William Dorrit. These people, fodder for Dickens' imagination, were on open display and ripe for incorporation into his stories; the desperate situation they found themselves in resulted in an attractiveness of character that Dickens could not resist, thus appealing to the writer while simultaneously appalling the man. It is this contradiction within Dickens that led him to some of the darkest and dingiest areas of London, a macabre fascination with the lowest levels of society that, as an artist, he could not resist; hence articles such as 'A Walk in a Workhouse' (*Household Words*, 27 May 1850). At one point in this article Dickens dismays that 'the dishonest felon is, in respect of cleanliness, order, diet, and accommodation, better provided for, and taken care of, than the honest pauper'. Clearly crime should not be rewarded, but here those who were making a nuisance enough of themselves were being taken in by the state while those who quietly struggled on were being ignored or simply 'moved on', like Jo the sweeper in *Bleak House*: not respectable enough to receive assistance, nor disreputable enough to warrant attention.

This idea of the wrong people being rewarded also resonates in the succeeding two articles, and it is worth keeping this in mind alongside the more popular concept of Dickens as the man of the people. He is regularly remembered and celebrated for his championing of the poor and for highlighting the woes befalling the underside of the city; but it should not be concluded from this that he was idealistic to the point of naivety. The two articles 'The Begging-letter Writer' (*Household Words*, 18 May 1850) and 'Tramps' (*All the Year Round*, 16 June 1860) demonstrate Dickens' cynicism towards those who preyed on the charitable feelings of others. Note that both articles describe people with genuine financial issues, but the reason why Dickens objects to them, and in some instances vilifies them, is the way they respond to these issues: they expect help without putting in any effort, they complain of the good fortunes of those who have worked industriously, and worse yet they try to trick others out of money rather than seek honest employment themselves. For Dickens this is unacceptable: those asking for help must *deserve* help; they must prove themselves worthy of the compassion and support of others by in turn showing themselves as pure, penitent or purposeful.

This issue comes particularly to the fore with the fairer sex. In 'Wapping Workhouse' Dickens considers the plight of women at the point of desperation, from those who commit suicide to those now in the workhouse, where he meets an equal mix of those who attract his sympathy and those who almost revel in their depravity. In both these instances and that of those who write letters or try to sell combs, it can be argued that they have as much right to help and assistance as those who appeal to Dickens' sensibility, but for Charles the priority in helping the many destitute in London was to start with the most deserving cases. This resulted in Urania Cottage, a project led by Dickens with the support (especially financially) of his friend Angela Burdett-Coutts (the full story of Dickens' involvement with this project is retold wonderfully in Jenny Hartley's *Charles Dickens and the House of Fallen Women*). Society's attitude to poor women was simple: needle-women were to be pitied, prostitutes were not. The circumstances that had led the latter to desperate measures were not recognised, the judgement was simply that they had failed morally, and were beyond redemption. Dickens saw beyond that, and Urania Cottage took in prostitutes (though the article does not specifically state this, referring instead to those 'young women from the streets'). Dickens carried out rigorous checks on every inmate, calling in favours from contacts in the police and prisons to verify their stories to ascertain whether they were first-time offenders, and more importantly whether their path to crime and deprivation had been unavoidable. The lucky few selected were treated to something quite new: a *home*; not an asylum, institute or sanctuary, but a place where redemption was offered without the judgement or condemnation they would expect elsewhere. Interestingly Dickens made an effort not to publicise his connection to the home (in contrast to many celebrities desperate to publicise their good work for charity); however he was keen to write about the home and spread its message, and having finally gained Burdett-Coutt's permission to do so, he wrote of Urania Cottage in 'Home for Homeless Women' (*Household Words*, 23 April 1853). The resulting piece gives a subjectively positive view of the project under the veil of objectivity, with Dickens continuing not to advertise his own involvement; even so, the achievement of the project is not to be overlooked: Dickens estimated that half the girls who stayed at Urania turned out to be successes, leading new lives abroad, getting married, starting families, and living free of 'the dragon pauperism' that had blighted their lives in England. Pessimists could of course counter this with the observation that half the girls were *not* successes; some took advantage, stealing clothes and running away, while others were kicked out when their frequent bad behaviour identified them as unsalvageable. But in a city where poverty was widespread, where Ignorance and Want worked their way through the streets, any success, any opportunity to allow a fellow human being to escape their fate and start afresh, was surely a victory.

And most importantly of all, Dickens had done *something*. Apathy was, as it is now, one of the greatest contributing factors to the continued suffering of others, and to simply shrug it off as unsolvable was not an acceptable answer for Dickens. In the closing article 'A December Vision' (*Household Words*, 14 December 1850), he articulates his feelings on this most forcefully, decrying those who look around them at things wrong in the world, but do nothing. It is a philosophy summarised by the motto displayed at Urania, and one which Dickens would have us remember today: 'Don't talk about it – do it!'

– *Pete Orford*, 2012

The Drouet Case

The Paradise at Tooting (20 January 1849)

When it first became known that a virulent and fatal epidemic had broken out in Mr Drouet's farming establishment for pauper children at Tooting, the comfortable flourish of trumpets usual on such occasions (Sydney Smith's admirable description of it will be fresh in the minds of many of our readers) was performed as a matter of course.[1] Of all similar establishments on earth, that at Tooting was the most admirable. Of all similar contractors on earth, Mr Drouet was the most disinterested, zealous, and unimpeachable. Of all the wonders ever wondered at, nothing perhaps had ever occurred more wonderful than the outbreak and rapid increase of a disorder so horrible, in a place so perfectly regulated. There was no warning of its approach. Nothing was less to be expected. The farmed children were slumbering in the lap of peace and plenty; Mr Drouet, the farmer, was slumbering with an easy conscience, but with one eye perpetually open, to keep watch upon the blessings he diffused, and upon the happy infants under his paternal charge; when, in a moment, the destroyer was upon them, and Tooting church-yard became too small for the piles of children's coffins that were carried out of this Elysium every day.

The learned coroner for the county of Surrey deemed it quite unnecessary to hold any inquests on these dead children, being as perfectly satisfied in his own mind that Mr Drouet's farm was the best of all possible farms, as ever the innocent Candide was that the chateau of the great Baron Thunder-ten Tronckh was the best of all possible chateaux.[2] Presuming that this learned functionary is amenable to some authority or other, and that he will be duly complimented on his sagacity, we will refer to the proceedings before a very different kind of coroner, Mr Wakley,[3] and his deputy Mr Mills. But that certain of the miserable little creatures removed from Tooting happened to die within Mr Wakley's jurisdiction, it is by no means unlikely that a committee might have sprung into existence, by this time, for presenting Mr Drouet with some magnificent testimonial, as a mark of public respect and sympathy.

Mr Wakley, however, being of little faith, holds inquests, and even manifests a disposition to institute a very searching inquiry into the causes of these horrors; rather thinking that such grievous effects must have some grievous causes. Remembering that there is a public institution called the 'Board of Health', Mr Wakley summons before him Dr Grainger, an inspector acting under that board, who has examined Mr Drouet's Elysium, and has drawn up a report concerning it.

It then comes out – truth is so perverse – that Mr Drouet is not altogether that golden farmer he was supposed to be. It appears that there is a little alloy in his composition. The 'extreme closeness, oppression, and foulness of air,' in that supposed heaven upon earth over which he presides, 'exceeds in offensiveness anything ever yet witnessed, by the inspector, in apartments in hospitals, or elsewhere, occupied by the sick.' He has a bad habit of putting four cholera patients in one bed. He has a weakness in respect of leaving the sick to take care of themselves, surrounded by every offensive, indecent, and barbarous circumstance that can aggravate the horrors of their condition and increase the dangers of infection. He is so ignorant, or so criminally careless, that he has taken none of the easy precautions, and provided himself with none of the simple remedies, expressly enjoined by the Board of Health in their official announcement published in the *Gazette*, and distributed all over the country. The experience of all the medical observers of cholera, in all parts of the world, is not in an instant overthrown by Mr Drouet's purity, for he had unfortunately one fortnight's warning of the impending danger, which he utterly disregarded. He has been admonished by the authorities to take only a certain number of unfortunates into his farm, and he increases that number immensely at his own pleasure, for his own profit. His establishment is crammed. It is in no respect a fit place for the reception of the throng shut up in it. The diet of the children is so unwholesome and insufficient, that they climb secretly over pailings, and pick out scraps of sustenance from the tubs of hog-wash. Their clothing by day, and their covering by night, are shamefully defective. Their rooms are cold, damp, dirty, and rotten. In a word, the age of miracles is past, and of all conceivable places in which pestilence might – or rather *must* – be expected to break out, and to make direful ravages, Mr Drouet's model farm stands foremost.

In addition to these various proofs of his mortal fallibility, Mr Drouet, even when he is told what to do to save life, has an awkward habit of prevaricating, and not doing it. He also bullies his assistants, in the inspector's presence, when they show an inclination to reveal disagreeable truths. He has a pleasant brother – a man of an amiable eccentricity – who besides being active, for all improper purposes, in the farm, is 'with difficulty restrained' from going to Kensington 'to thrash the Guardians' of that Union for proposing to remove their children! The boys under Mr Drouet's fostering protection are habitually knocked down, beaten, and brutally used. They are put on short diet if they complain. They are 'very lean and emaciated.' Mr Drouet's system is admirable, but it entails upon them such slight evils as 'wasting of limbs, debility, boils; &c.,' and a more dreadful aggravation of the itch than a medical witness of great experience has ever beheld in thirty years' practice. A kick, which would be nothing to a child in sound health, becomes, under Mr Drouet's course of management, a serious wound. Boys who were intelligent before going to Drouet, lose their animation afterwards (so swears a Guardian) and become fools. The surgeon of St Pancras reported, five months ago, of the excellent Mr Drouet, 'that a great deal of severity, not to use a harsh term' – but why not a harsh term, surgeon, if the occasion require it? – 'has been exercised by the masters in authority, as well as some we presume, out of authority,' meaning, we presume, the amiably eccentric brother. Everything, in short, that Mr Drouet does, or causes to be done, or suffers to be done, is vile, vicious, and cruel. All this is distinctly in proof before the coroner's jury, and therefore we see no reason to abstain from summing it up.

But there is blame elsewhere; and though it cannot diminish the heavy amount of blame that rests on this sordid contractor's head, there is great blame elsewhere. The parish authorities who sent these children to such a place, and, seeing them in it, left them there, and showed no resolute determination to reform it altogether, are culpable in the highest degree. The Poor-Law Inspector who visited this place, and did not, in the strongest terms, condemn it, is not less culpable. The Poor-Law Commissioners, if they had the power to issue positive orders for its better management (a point which is, however, in question), were as culpable as any of the rest.

It is wonderful to see how those who, by slurring the matter when they should have been active in it, have become, in some sort, *participes criminis*, desire to make the best of it, even now.[4] The Poor-Law Inspector thinks that the issuing of an order by the Poor-Law Commissioners, prohibiting boards of guardians from sending children to such an institution, would have been 'a very strong measure.' As if very strong cases required very weak measures, or there were no natural affinity between the measure and the case! He certainly did object to the children sleeping three in a bed, and Mr Drouet afterwards told him he had reduced the number to two – its increase to four when the disease was raging, being, we suppose, a special sanitary arrangement. He did not make any recommendation as to ventilation. He did not call the children privately before him, to inquire how they were treated. He considers the dietary a fair dietary – IF *proper quantities were given where no precise quantity is specified*. He thinks that, with care, the premises might have been accommodated without danger to health, IF *all the accommodation, on the premises had been judiciously applied*. As though a man should say he felt convinced he could live pretty comfortably on the top of the Monument, IF a handsome suite of furnished apartments were constructed there expressly for him, and a select circle came up to dinner every day!

These children were farmed to Mr Drouet at four shillings and sixpence a week each; and some of the officials seem to set store by its being a great deal of money, and to think exoneration lies in that. It may be a very sufficient sum, considering that Mr Drouet was entitled to the profits of the children's work, besides: but this seems to us to be no part of the question. If the payment had been fourteen and sixpence a week each, the blame of leaving the children to Mr Drouet's tender mercies without sufficient protection, and of leaving Mr Drouet to make his utmost profit without sufficient check, would have been exactly the same. When a man keeps his horse at livery, he does not take the corn for granted, because he pays five-and-twenty shillings a week. In the history of this calamity, one undoubted predisposing cause was insufficient clothing. What says Mr William Robert James, solicitor and clerk to the Board of Guardians of the Holborn Union, on that head? Mr Drouet '*told him in conversation* (!) that the four and sixpence a week would include clothing. *No particular description of clothing was mentioned.*' Is it any wonder that the flannel petticoats worn by the miserable female children, in the severest weather of this winter, could be – as was publicly stated in another metropolitan union a few days ago – 'read through?'

This same Mr James produces minutes of visits made by deputations of guardians to the Tooting Paradise. Thus:

> As regards the complaint of Hannah Sleight, as to the insufficiency of food, we believe it to be unfounded. Elizabeth Male having complained that on her recent visit she found her children in a dirty state her children had our particular attention, and we beg to state that there was no just cause of complaint on her part.

It being clear to the meanest capacity that Elizabeth Male's children not being dirty then, never could by possibility have been dirty at any antecedent time.

But it appears that this identical James, solicitor and clerk to the Board of Guardians of the Holborn Union, had a valuable system of his own for eliciting the truth, which was, to ask the boys in Mr Drouet's presence if they had anything to complain of, and when they answered 'Yes,' to recommend that they should be instantly horsewhipped. We learn this, from the following extraordinary minute of one of these official visits:

> We beg to report to the board our having on Tuesday, the 9th of May, visited Mr Drouet's establishment to ascertain the state of the children belonging to this union. We were there at the time of dinner being supplied, and in our opinion the meat provided was good, but the potatoes were bad. We visited the school-rooms, dormitories, and workshops. *Everything appeared clean and comfortable*, *yet we are of opinion that the new sleeping resins for infants on the ground floor have a very unhealthy smell.* The girls belonging to the Union looked very well. *The boys appeared sickly*, which induced us to question them as to whether they had any cause of complaint as to supply of food or otherwise. About forty of them held up their hands to intimate their dissatisfaction, upon which Mr Drouet's conduct became violent. He called the boys liars, described some that had held up their hands as the worst boys in the school, and said that if he had done them justice, he would have followed out the suggestion of Mr James, and well thrashed them. (Laughter.) We then began to question the boys individually, and some of them complained of not having sufficient bread at their breakfast. Whilst pressing the inquiry, Mr Drouet's conduct became more violent. He said we were acting unfairly in the mode of inquiry, that we ought to be satisfied of his character without such proceedings, and that

> we had no right to pursue the inquiry in the way we were doing, and that he would be glad to get rid of the children. To avoid further altercation we left, not having fully completed the object of our visit.

If Mr Drouet was sincere in saying he would be glad to get rid of the children, he must be in a very complacent frame of mind at present when he has succeeded in getting rid, for ever, of so many. But the general complacency, on the occasions of these visits, is marvellous. Hear Mr Winch, one of the guardians of the poor for the Holborn Union, who was one of the visiting party at the Tooting Paradise on this 9th of May:

> I was in company with Mr Mayes and Mr Rebbeck. The children were at dinner. They were all standing; I was informed they never sit at their meals. I tasted the meat, and I cut open about 100 potatoes at different tables, *none of which were fit to eat*. They were black and diseased. I told Mr Drouet the potatoes were very bad. He replied that they cost him 7*l*. a ton. The children had no other vegetables. *I told Mr Drouet I should give them other food. He made no reply. I also told Mr Drouet I thought the newly-erected rooms, smelt unhealthy*. Mr Mayes said it was a pity when he was building he had not made the rooms higher; when *Mr Drouet said he would have enough to do if he paid attention to everybody*. We went through some of the sleeping-rooms, which appeared very clean. The girls looked well; but the boys, who were mustered in the school-room, appeared very sickly and unhealthy. *Mr Drouet, his brother, and the schoolmaster, were present*. Mr Rebbeck said to the boys, 'Now, if you have anything to complain of – want of food, or anything else – hold up your hands;' and from thirty to forty held up their hands. *Mr Drouet became very violent*, and said we were treating him in an ungentlemanly manner; he said that some of the boys who had held up their

hands were liars, and scoundrels, and rascals. He said we were using him very unfairly; *that his character was at stake*; and, if we had anything to complain of, that was not the way to proceed. *One of the boys whom I questioned told me they had not bread enough either for breakfast or supper; and, on comparing their dietary with that in our workhouse, I think such is the case.* In consequence of the confusion, we left Mr Drouet's without signing the visitors' book. I did not make any motion in the Board of Guardians for the removal of the children. I again visited Mr Drouet's establishment on the 30th of May. The potatoes were then of excellent quality. *I went into the pantry, and was surprised to find the bread was not weighed out. We weigh it out in the union, as we find that is the only way to give satisfaction.* The loaves at Mr Drouet's were cut into sixteen pieces without being weighed. I saw no supply of salt in the dining-room, but some of the boys who had salt in bags were bartering their salt for potatoes. *I did not ask the children whether they had been punished in consequence of what had taken place at my previous visit.* We were in the establishment for an hour and a half or two hours on the 30th. *We then expressed our satisfaction at what we witnessed.* We made no further inquiry as to what had occurred on our previous visit. I made no suggestion to the board for the improvement of the dietary. *We had no means of ascertaining that the children received the amount of food mentioned in the diet-table.*

But we expressed our satisfaction at what we witnessed. Oh dear yes. Our unanimity was delightful. Nobody complained. The boys had had ample encouragement to complain. They had seen Mr Drouet standing glowering by, on the previous occasion. They had heard him break out about liars, and scoundrels, and rascals. They had understood that his precious character – immeasurably more precious than the existence of any number of pauper children – was at stake. They had had the benefit of a little fatherly advice and caution from him, in the interval. They were in a position, moral and physical, to be high-spirited, bold, and open. Yet not a boy complained. We went home to our Holborn Union, rejoicing. Our clerk was in tip-top spirits about the thrashing joke. Everything was comfortable and pleasant. Of all places in the world, how could the cholera ever break out, after this, in Mr Drouet's Paradise at Tooting!

If we had been left to the so-much vaunted self-government, the question might have been unanswered still, and the Drouet testimonial might have been in full vigour. But the Board of Health – an institution of which every day's experience attests in some new form the value and importance has settled the question. Plainly thus:– the cholera, or some unusually malignant form of typhus assimilating itself to that disease, broke out in Mr Drouet's farm for children, because it was brutally conducted, vilely kept, preposterously inspected, dishonestly defended, a disgrace to a Christian community, and a stain upon a civilised land.

The Tooting Farm (27 January 1849)

On Tuesday last the coroner's jury, after a long inquiry before Mr Wakley, returned a verdict of manslaughter against the Tooting Farmer, coupled with an expression of their regret at the defects of the Poor-law Act, and of their hope that establishments similar to that at Tooting would soon cease to exist.

Nothing came out in the further progress of the inquiry to soften those results of evidence which we summed up generally last week. The new testimony did anything but weaken the case against the person now criminally inculpated. On the contrary, the physical deterioration of the surviving children, as a body, was more affectingly and convincingly shown than before. What good legal assistance could do for the defence, was done, but it could do nothing. What deplorable shifts and attempts at evasion on the part of an educated witness could do on the same side, was also done. But it could do nothing either.

We observe that one metropolitan Board of Guardians considers itself ill-used by the public comments that have been made on this case, and is about to enter on a voluntary defence of itself. Any individual or body of individuals made the subject of uncomplimentary newspaper remark, *is* ill-used as a matter of course. It never was otherwise. The precedents are numerous. Mr Thurtell was very bitter on this point, and so was Mr Greenacre. But while we recognise a broad distinction between the culpability of those who consigned hundreds of children to this hateful place, too easily satisfied by formal, periodical visitation of it, – and the guilt of its administrator, who knew it at all hours and times, at its worst as well as at its best, and who drove a dangerous and cruel traffic, for his own profit, at his own peril, – we must take leave to repeat that the Board of Guardians concerned are grossly in the wrong. The plain truth is, that they took for granted what they should have thoroughly sifted and ascertained. A certain establishment for the reception of pauper children exists. One Board of Guardians sends its children there; other Boards of Guardians follow in its wake, like sheep. We will assume that the existing accommodation in their Unions was insufficient for the reception of these children. For aught we know, it may, in the case of the Saint Pancras workhouse for example, have been perfectly inadequate. But that is no reason for sending them to Tooting, and no ground of defence in having sent them there. The sending them to Norfolk Island, or the banks of the Niger, might be justified as well by the same logic.

We have no intention of prejudging a case which is now to be brought to issue before a criminal court. It will be decided upon the law, and upon the evidence, and there is not the least fear that the general humanity will unjustly prejudice the party impeached. That is not at all a common vice of such a trial in England. What we desire to do, is to point out in a few words why we hold it to be particularly desirable that this case, in all its relations, should be rigidly dealt with upon its own merits; and why that vague disposition to smooth over the things that be, which sometimes creeps into the most important English proceedings, should, in this instance of all others, have no pin's-point of place to rest upon.

In town and country, for some months past, we have been trying and punishing with necessary severity certain seditious men who did their utmost to incite the discontented to disturbance of the public peace.[5] We have, within the last year, counted our special constables by tens of thousands, and our loyal addresses to the throne by tens of scores. All these demonstrations have been necessary, but some of them have been sad necessities, and, on the subsidence of the natural indignation of the moment, have not left much occasion for triumph.

The chartist leaders who are now undergoing their various sentences in various prisons, found the mass of their audience among the discontented poor. The foremost of them had not the plea of want to urge for themselves; but their misrepresentations were addressed to the toiling multitudes, on whom social inequalities impossible to be avoided, and complicated commercial circumstances difficult to be explained to them, pressed heavily. There is no doubt that among this numerous class, chartist principles are rife; that wherever the class is found in a large amount, there, also, is a great intensity of discontent. There are few poor workingmen in the kingdom who *might* not find themselves next year, next month, next week, in the position of those fathers whose children were sent to Tooting; and there are probably very few poor working-men who have not thought 'this might be my child's case, to-morrow.'

No opportunity of doing something towards the education of such men in the conviction that the State is unfeignedly mindful of them, and truly anxious to redress their tangible and obvious wrongs, could be plainer than that which now arises. If the system of farming pauper children cannot exist without the danger of another Tooting Farm being weeded by the grisly hands of Want, Disease, and Death, let it be now abolished. If the Poor Law, as it stands, be not efficient for the prevention of such inhuman evils, let it be now rendered more efficient. If it has unfortunately happened, though by no man's deliberate intention or malignity – as who can doubt it has? – that the children of sundry poor men and women have been carried to untimely graves, who might have lived and thriven, let there be seen a resolute determination that the like shall never happen any more. It is not only even-handed justice, but it is clear, straightforward policy. It is the correction of widely-spread and artfully-fomented prejudice, dissatisfaction, and suspicion. It is to challenge and to win the confidence of the poor man on his tenderest point, and at his own fire-side.

But to waste the occasion in play with foolscap and red tape; to bewilder all these listening ears with mere official gabble about Boards, and Inspectors, and Guardians, and responsibility, and non-responsibility, and divided responsibility, and powers, and clauses, and sections, and chapters, until the remedy is crushed to pieces in a mill of words; will be to swell the mischief to an extent that is incalculable. There are scores of heads in the mills of Lancashire and the shops of Birmingham, sufficiently confused already by something more perplexing than the rattling of looms or the beating of hammers. Such dazed men must be spoken to distinctly. They will hear then, and hear aright. Let the debtor and creditor account between the governors and the governed, be kept in a fair, bold hand, that all may read; and the governed will soon read it for themselves, and dispense with the interpreters who are paid by chartist clubs.

A Recorder's Charge (3 March 1849)

People who went to see Mr. Catlin's party of Indians at the Egyptian Hall, were in general mightily entertained to observe how necessary 'medicine,' or mystery, was to the greater part of their proceedings; and how impossible the red men considered it to set hopefully about any grave undertaking without divers preliminary conjurations from the 'medicine man.'[6] Really, the custom obtains quite as extensively among the white men of England. What an enormous amount of Medicine is held to be necessary, among us, before we can set about the plainest piece of business! Worse still. In some cases – as in that of the church, for example – our Medicine men differ violently among themselves, and in a conflict of Medicine set all England by the ears, when it is only desirous to say its prayers in peace. In parliament, besides a great deal of very indifferent Medicine constantly practised and never varying, we have the standard Medicine of a select committee, which is one of its most perplexing and complicated mysteries, and very bad Medicine indeed. At court we have ceremonies far more ridiculous than anything in the Ojibbeway code of *etiquette*.[7] In law, we have a solemn jingling of words and phrases which is the most bewildering and unmeaning Medicine of all.

The grand jury, coming into court at the Old Bailey on Monday last to be regaled with a little Medicine of this latter kind, were addressed by the learned Recorder for the City of London, who, as Medicine man, danced round and round them, and the general question of the Tooting case, in the following wild manner:

The charge in question was made against the keeper of an establishment for the reception of pauper children, at Tooting, *and he was accused of having caused the deaths of no less than four children, by a degree of criminal neglect, in not giving them proper food, by crowding them together in an unwholesome atmosphere, and a general inattention to those precautions which were necessary to preserve a number of children, placed together under such circumstances, in a state of ordinary bodily health*. It appeared that several parishes, acting under proper authority, had sent a number of children to the establishment in question, where they were placed under the charge of the defendant, who was to receive a stipulated price per head for the children. The exact number that was so received did not exactly appear, *but there was no doubt that it was larger than the capabilities of the establishment could properly provide for, and that the children were consequently crowded together in a manner likely to be injurious to their health, and predispose them to the attack of any epidemic or contagious disease.* The indictment would probably allege that it was the duty of the defendant, by the contract he had entered into, to supply proper food and clothing, and to take proper precautions to preserve the health of the children placed under his charge, and that he had criminally neglected to perform that duty. The depositions were very voluminous, and he was bound to say that they contained many statements which were not legally admissible, and which would not be received or admitted by a judge. A good deal of the matter consisted of hearsay evidence, and of conclusions drawn by parties who did not state any facts upon which those conclusions were founded. The cause of the deaths appeared to be clearly proved to be cholera, and by the depositions it appeared that there had been a good deal of speculation as to how the disease of cholera was occasioned, and how far it might have been prevented, in the present instance, supposing more food had been given to the deceased children, and they had been provided with more clothes and greater comforts. *In an ordinary case of manslaughter*, the cause of death was generally distinctly alleged against the party accused, but in this case the offence which appeared to be imputed to the defendant was, that by a certain course of improper treatment he had predisposed the system of the deceased children to receive the disease, and had rendered them peculiarly liable to be attacked by the disorder. The important question, however, was, *what act* had been done by the defendant that had conduced to the death of the deceased.

The Recorder talks about 'an ordinary case of manslaughter,' as if there were nothing whatever in the Tooting case to make it an *extra*ordinary one. The question is, *what act* has been done by the defendant to conduce to the death of the deceased! Is it? Or does the question extend itself into a series of acts, no one among them in itself perhaps involving the terrible catastrophe so widely known, but all, taken together, involving that degree of gross neglect of ordinary precaution for the safety of human life, which constitutes one form of manslaughter? Suppose another kind of 'farmer,' being skipper of a ship, had taken on board for his profit an unheard-of number of apprentices, and 'by a degree of criminal neglect in not giving them proper food, by crowding them together in an unwholesome atmosphere, and a general inattention to those precautions which are necessary to preserve them,' had so reduced and wasted those apprentices that after certain weeks of this ill-treatment scurvy or erysipelas broke out among them, and swept numbers of them away. Does the Recorder mean to say that to sustain a charge of manslaughter against that man, it would be necessary to prove any one specific act on his part amounting to inoculation for scurvy or erysipelas? 'Did the defendant do *any act*.' 'They must see *what act* had been done.' Again and again the Recorder jingles and juggles with this phrase. 'Under these circumstances he would ask them who could say that the defendant was the cause of the children being attacked by cholera, and yet they must be satisfied that this was the case before the defendant would be amenable to the present charge.' But supposing the grand jury had taken it into their heads to ask the medical witnesses whether, the children being attacked by cholera, the defendant was the cause of its being physically impossible that they could recover, in that lazar-house which was his Mint, – would they have travelled very far out of the strict justice of the case?

'The question is *what* act has been done.' This is the great Medicine for the Grand Jury. Let us test the Medicine. Here is a proclamation, we will imagine, published with the sanction and authority of the Crown, and made notorious in every newspaper and channel of information, cautioning all engine-drivers on railways, that by reason of some uncommon condition of the atmosphere they are liable to a new class of fatal accidents; enjoining them, upon the first appearance of certain warnings which usually precede these accidents, and which are plainly described, to stop; and instructing them with what remedies to be provided beforehand, at the cost of a few pence, and how to use them, on the instant, for the protection of all under their charge. One engine-driver, having in his care the largest and the worst-appointed train in the kingdom, which is very profitable to him, sets these instructions at defiance, disregards the warnings which have been foretold to him, and which manifest themselves to his senses beyond all question, and going on headlong, comes to a crash, and destroys one hundred and fifty-five passengers,* – are we to be told that before he could be tried for the manslaughter of four of these unfortunates, it would be necessary to show that he had put a luggage-van across the railway, or a hundredweight of gunpowder into the boiler?

Is it easy to believe that the parallel case to this, the Recorder utterly dismisses from his and the grand jury's consideration? In all these wanderings and repetitions of words about ordinary cases of manslaughter, there is not one word of reference to the extraordinary circumstances of the time; to the bounden duty of the keeper of such an establishment to adapt his arrangements in some degree to the peculiar peril of the time; to the circular of the Board of Health, expressly addressed to masters of asylums, schools, workhouses, and all such institutions, warning them not to be defective, in all the respects in which this place was most defective; to the total neglect of that circular in this particular case; to the appearance of the premonitory symptoms one fortnight before the breaking out of the disease; and to their being passed over with the same shameful indifference and neglect which characterised the whole administration of

* The registered number of deaths from cholera at the Tooting Establishment to January 20th.

the house! On all these vital points of the case, there is not one word in the Recorder's charge. Nay, the Recorder deems it a great point in the defendant's favour 'that the same treatment had been pursued for a period of six years without any such result taking place;' and really is as cool upon it as if it were notorious to the whole world that the cholera had been among us all that time!

The magnates of the city have been taking very high flights into the regions of Noodledom lately,[8] borne aloft upon the balmy air of Smithfield; and it would seem as if the Recorder were dutifully meting out his Medicine by the standard at Guildhall.

In the same spirit he talks about there having been no complaint with reference to the food generally, down to the month of June last, 'when there was some complaint with regard to the potatoes.' As if there had been no difficulty of complaint! As if nobody remembered anything of the defendant's conduct to the boys when they *did* complain! As if the surviving children had never been weighed against other pauper children, and found in an extreme state of physical deterioration! As if there were no evidence of dire and gnawing hunger having been among them habitually!

The Recorder's speech might be a good enough address for the defendant's counsel, but it is a very bad charge from the judicial bench. It could not have been much more out of place at Covent Garden Market the other day, when the modest Mr. Charles Cochrane and his literary friend Mr. G.W.M. Reynolds, author of the *Mysteries of London*, and of the Revolution of Trafalgar Square, appeared upon the hustings in hopes to enclose and cultivate for themselves a snug little farm of a grievance, out of the Tooting paradise.[9] It is so peculiarly the misfortune of these illustrious patriots to damage and debase any cause with which they connect themselves, that we should hail their expatriation for life on any constitutional grounds, with unbounded satisfaction.

Although we cannot but lament that the Poor-Law Amendment Act did not invest the Commissioners with due powers for the government of such a place as that at Tooting, we are glad to find, from Mr. Baines's explanation in the House of Commons, that such powers will now be conferred upon them. The most important provisions of the Out-door Pauper's Bill appear to be, that the Commissioners will henceforth prescribe rules for the management of such houses (of which there are but few in existence); that they will revise the contracts made between the guardians and the contractors, and stipulate for certain conditions, with power of enforcing penalties for non-fulfilment; that they will have the power of summarily dismissing the contractors; and that they will have 'very effective powers of visitation.' Nothing is more necessary than these last. If the Sanitary Commission had not fortunately possessed (under the Removal of Nuisances Bill) the right of visiting Tooting without invitation, we should probably never have had Mr. Grainger's Report.

That it is not proposed to invest the Poor-Law Commission with these new powers before they are needed, is now a trite truth, which we cannot better confirm than by a short extract from a valuable, thoroughly-informed, and most useful publication, the *Journal of Public Health*. Let us premise that we allow *one thousand feet* of cubic air to every felon in his prison:

> Let us set aside all the inhumanity and brutal indifference which have been brought out in evidence – on this Tooting case – 'the hunger and thirst, the cold, the ill-treatment, the uncleanliness, the diseases of filth and neglect, the itch, scald heads, the sore eyes, the running tetters, the scrofulous affections of the joints, and abscesses, the thin shanks and pot bellies, the diseased bowels, the foundation for the consumption of coming years, which were inflicted on these much-abused children – and judge of the system by the regard paid to the primary want of LIFE under all

conditions – *the supply of fresh air*. We are told that the children had not quite 136 cubic feet of respirable air for each child, or an amount equal to what could be contained in a box five feet two inches every way. This supply would preserve life for eight hours, when the outraged laws of life would resolve the living frame into dead matter. In the boys' schoolroom, occupied for three hours twice a day, there were thirty-seven cubic feet of air for each boy!

Will all our Medicine-men insist, like the Recorder, on having the Tooting tragedy in 'one act,' or will any of them be content to read it in fifty?

The Verdict for Drouet (23 April 1849)

The peculiarity of this verdict is, that while it has released the accused from the penalties of the law it has certainly not released him from the guilt of the charge. The prosecution, badly as it was conducted, established what was alleged against Drouet. The hunger and thirst were proved; the bad food, and the insufficient clothing; the cold, the ill-treatment, the uncleanliness; the diseases generated by filth and neglect; the itch (much to Mr Baron Platt's amusement), the scald heads, the sore eyes, the scrofulous affections, the pot bellies, and the thin shanks. All were proved. We give a thousand cubic feet of respirable air to every felon in his prison, and each child in Drouet's prison had little more than a tenth part so much. They were half-starved, and more than half-suffocated. A terrible malady broke out, and a hundred and fifty perished. It was in evidence that every indecent and revolting incident that could aggravate the slightest illness, or increase the horrors of the most dangerous infection, existed in the establishment for which Drouet was responsible, when disease appeared there. But it was not satisfactorily proved that the disease might not have killed as many without such help, and therefore Mr Baron Platt very properly told the jury that the case had broken down.

The legal point arose upon that part of the indictment which charged Drouet with having neglected the duty of a right mode of treatment to the child named in it; in support of which the fact of the constitutional energy of the child having been so reduced by his management as to render it unable to resist the particular disease, was relied upon as having brought Drouet within the penalties of man slaughter. But the judge, setting aside this argument as inapplicable to the case, directed an acquittal on the ground that there had been no evidence adduced to show that the child was ever, at any time, in such a state of health as to render it probable he would have recovered from the malady but for the treatment of the defendant.

The extent of the wrong, in other words, precluded the remedy. For who, in such a crowd of children, could have singled out one poor child at any time, to say whether he was well or ill? The deputy-matron of the workhouse from which he went to Tooting, and to which he returned to die, could only say of the whole hundred and fifty-six that came back to her on the same night, that 'they were not so stout and healthy as when they went to Mr Drouet's.' No – she was certain they were not. 'They were very sore in their bodies, and had sore feet, and there were wounds on different parts of their persons'; and some lived, and some died, and among the latter was little Andrews. That is the whole humble history. There was no doctor to examine the children when they left, or when they returned; and evidence of half the wickedness of the 'farm' was rejected, because one wretched little figure could not always be visibly separated from a crowd exactly like himself, and shown as he contended with horrors to which all were equally exposed. We are not objecting to the verdict on these grounds, but explaining it. The scruples of the law were quite justifiable and right; though we might have been better pleased to see them enforced, in the particular case, with less tenderness for Drouet and more concern for his victims.

Mr Baron Platt declared himself early. The prosecution being less strongly represented than the defence, he took the very first opportunity of siding with the stronger. Witnesses that required encouragement, he brow-beat; and witnesses that could do without it, he insulted or ridiculed. Medical men are not famous for the clearness of their testimony at any time, and such questions from the bench as whether hunger and the itch were connected, and whether cholera was producible by the itch, did not put them more at their ease. Of course there was laughter at the facetiousness. There was also zealous applause, with which the prisoner signified his concurrence by tapping with his hand in front of the dock.

Nevertheless the trial cannot be read without much anguish of heart. The inexpressible sadness of its details is not relieved by Mr Baron Platt's jocoseness. One little touch came out in the evidence of a peculiarly affecting kind, such as the masters of pathos have rarely excelled in fiction. The learned baron was not moved by it; naturally enough, for he had not the least notion what it meant.

> Mary Harris, examined by Mr Clarkson: I am a nurse at Holborn union workhouse, and went to the Royal Free Hospital, Gray's-inn road. I recollect Andrews coming with the other boys. He was not well. I gave him some milk and bread.
>
> Mr Clarkson: *Did he eat his bread?*
>
> Witness: *No; he held up his head, and said, 'Oh, nurse, what a big bit of bread this is!'*
>
> Baron Platt: *It was too much for him, I suppose?*
>
> Witness: *He could not eat it.*

'*Oh nurse!*' says the poor little fellow, with an eager sense that what he had longed for had come too late, '*What a big bit of bread this is!*' Yes, Mr Baron Platt, it is clear that it was too much for him. His head was lifted up for an instant, but it sank again. He could not but be full of wonder and pleasure that the big bit of bread had come, though he could not eat it. An English poet, in the days when poetry and poverty were inseparable companions, received a bit of bread in somewhat similar circumstances which proved too much for him, and he died in the act of swallowing it. The difference is hardly worth pointing out. The pauper child had not even strength for the effort which choked the pauper poet.

Drouet was 'affected to tears' as he left the dock. It might be gratitude for his escape, or it might be grief that his occupation was put an end to. For no one doubts that the child-farming system is effectually broken up by this trial. And every one must rejoice that a trade which derived its profits from the deliberate torture and neglect of a class the most innocent on earth, as well as the most wretched and defenceless, can never on any pretence be resumed.

The Pawnbroker's Shop

Of the numerous receptacles for misery and distress with which the streets of London unhappily abound, there are, perhaps, none which present such striking scenes as the pawnbrokers' shops. The very nature and description of these places occasions their being but little known, except to the unfortunate beings whose profligacy or misfortune drives them to seek the temporary relief they offer. The subject may appear, at first sight, to be anything but an inviting one, but we venture on it nevertheless, in the hope that, as far as the limits of our present paper are concerned, it will present nothing to disgust even the most fastidious reader.

There are some pawnbrokers' shops of a very superior description. There are grades in pawning as in everything else, and distinctions must be observed even in poverty. The aristocratic Spanish cloak and the plebeian calico shirt, the silver fork and the flat iron, the muslin cravat and the Belcher neckerchief, would but ill assort together; so, the better sort of pawnbroker calls himself a silver-smith, and decorates his shop with handsome trinkets and expensive jewellery, while the more humble money-lender boldly advertises his calling, and invites observation. It is with pawnbrokers' shops of the latter class, that we have to do. We have selected one for our purpose, and will endeavour to describe it.

The pawnbroker's shop is situated near Drury Lane, at the corner of a court, which affords a side entrance for the accommodation of such customers as may be desirous of avoiding the observation of the passers-by, or the chance of recognition in the public street. It is a low, dirty-looking, dusty shop, the door of which stands always doubtfully, a little way open: half inviting, half repelling the hesitating visitor, who, if he be as yet uninitiated, examines one of the old garnet brooches in the window for a minute or two with affected eagerness, as if he contemplated making a purchase; and then looking cautiously round to ascertain that no one watches him, hastily slinks in: the door closing of itself after him, to just its former width. The shop front and the window-frames bear evident marks of having been once painted; but, what the colour was originally, or at what date it was probably laid on, are at this remote period questions which may be asked, but cannot be answered. Tradition states that the transparency in the front door, which displays at night three red balls on a blue ground, once bore also, inscribed in graceful waves, the words, 'Money advanced on plate, jewels, wearing apparel, and every description of property,' but a few illegible hieroglyphics are all that now remain to attest the fact. The plate and jewels would seem to have disappeared, together with the announcement, for the articles of stock, which are displayed in some profusion in the window, do not include any very valuable luxuries of either kind. A few old china cups; some modern vases, adorned with paltry paintings of three Spanish cavaliers playing three Spanish guitars; or a party of boors carousing: each boor with one leg painfully elevated in the air, by way of expressing his perfect freedom and gaiety; several sets of chessmen, two or three flutes, a few fiddles, a round-eyed portrait staring in astonishment from a very dark ground; some gaudily-bound prayer-books and testaments, two rows of silver watches quite as clumsy and almost as large as Ferguson's first;[10] numerous old-fashioned table and tea spoons, displayed, fan-like, in half-dozens; strings of coral with great broad gilt snaps; cards of rings and brooches, fastened and labelled separately, like the insects in the British Museum; cheap silver penholders and snuff-boxes, with a masonic star, complete the jewellery department; while five or six beds in smeary clouded ticks, strings of blankets and sheets, silk and cotton handkerchiefs, and wearing apparel of every description, form the more useful, though even less ornamental, part, of the articles exposed for sale. An extensive collection of planes, chisels, saws, and other carpenters' tools, which have been pledged, and never redeemed, form the foreground of the picture; while the large frames full of ticketed bundles, which are dimly seen through the dirty casement up-stairs – the squalid neighbourhood – the adjoining houses, straggling, shrunken, and rotten, with one or two filthy, unwholesome-looking heads thrust out of every window, and old red pans and stunted plants exposed on the tottering parapets, to the manifest hazard of the heads of the passers-by – the noisy men loitering under the archway at the corner of the court, or about the gin-shop next door – and their wives patiently standing on the curb-stone, with large baskets of cheap vegetables slung round them for sale, are its immediate auxiliaries.

If the outside of the pawnbroker's shop be calculated to attract the attention, or excite the interest, of the speculative pedestrian, its interior cannot fail to produce the same effect in an increased degree. The front door, which we have before noticed, opens into the common shop, which is the resort of all those customers whose habitual acquaintance with such scenes renders them indifferent to the observation of their companions in poverty. The side door opens into a small passage from which some half-dozen doors (which may be secured on the inside by bolts) open into a corresponding number of little dens, or closets, which face the counter. Here, the more timid or respectable portion of the crowd shroud themselves from the notice of the remainder, and patiently wait until the gentleman behind the counter, with the curly black hair, diamond ring, and double silver watch-guard, shall feel disposed to favour them with his notice – a consummation which depends considerably on the temper of the aforesaid gentleman for the time being.

At the present moment, this elegantly-attired individual is in the act of entering the duplicate he has just made out, in a thick book: a process from which he is diverted occasionally, by a conversation he is carrying on with another young man similarly employed at a little distance from him, whose allusions to 'that last bottle of soda-water last night,' and 'how regularly round my hat he felt himself when the young 'ooman gave 'em in charge,' would appear to refer to the consequences of some stolen joviality of the preceding evening. The customers generally, however, seem unable to participate in the amusement derivable from this source, for an old sallow-looking woman, who has been leaning with both arms on the counter with a small bundle before her, for half an hour previously, suddenly interrupts the conversation by addressing the jewelled shopman – 'Now, Mr. Henry, do make haste, there's a good soul, for my two grandchildren's locked up at home, and I'm afeer'd of the fire.' The shopman slightly raises his head, with an air of deep abstraction, and resumes his entry with as much deliberation as if he were engraving. 'You're in a hurry, Mrs. Tatham, this ev'nin', an't you?' is the only notice he deigns to take, after the lapse of five minutes or so. 'Yes, I am indeed, Mr. Henry; now, do serve me next, there's a good creetur. I wouldn't worry you, only it's all along o' them botherin' children.' 'What have you got here?' inquires the shopman, unpinning the bundle – 'old concern, I suppose – pair o' stays and a petticut. You must look up somethin' else, old 'ooman; I can't lend you anything more upon them; they're completely worn out by this time, if it's only by putting in, and taking out again, three times a week.' 'Oh! you're a rum un, you are,' replies the old woman, laughing extremely, as in duty bound; 'I wish I'd got the gift of the gab like you; see if I'd be up the spout so often then! No, no; it an't the petticut; it's a child's frock and a beautiful silk ankecher, as belongs to my husband.[11] He gave four shillin' for it, the werry same blessed day as he broke his arm.' – 'What do you want upon these?' inquires Mr. Henry, slightly glancing at the articles, which in all probability are old acquaintances. 'What do you want upon these?' – 'Eighteenpence.' – 'Lend you ninepence.' – 'Oh, make it a shillin'; there's a dear – do now?' – 'Not another farden.' – 'Well, I suppose I must take it.' The duplicate is made out, one ticket pinned on the parcel, the other given to the old woman; the parcel is flung carelessly down into a corner, and some other customer prefers his claim to be served without further delay.

The choice falls on an unshaven, dirty, sottish-looking fellow, whose tarnished paper-cap, stuck negligently over one eye, communicates an additionally repulsive expression to his very uninviting countenance. He was enjoying a little relaxation from his sedentary pursuits a quarter of an hour ago, in kicking his wife up the court. He has come to redeem some tools:– probably to complete a job with, on account of which he has already received some money, if his inflamed countenance and drunken staggers may be taken as evidence of the fact. Having waited some little time, he makes his presence known by venting his ill-humour on a ragged urchin, who, being unable to bring his face on a level with the counter by any other process, has employed himself in climbing up, and then hooking himself on with his elbows – an uneasy perch, from which he has fallen at intervals, generally alighting on the toes of the person in his immediate vicinity. In the present case, the unfortunate little wretch has received a cuff which sends him reeling to this door; and the donor of the blow is immediately the object of general indignation.

'What do you strike the boy for, you brute?' exclaims a slip-shod woman, with two flat irons in a little basket. 'Do you think he's your wife, you willin?' 'Go and hang yourself!' replies the gentleman addressed, with a drunken look of savage stupidity, aiming at the same time a blow at the woman which fortunately misses its object. 'Go and hang yourself; and wait till I come and cut you down.' – 'Cut you down,' rejoins the woman, 'I wish I had the cutting of you up, you wagabond! (loud.) Oh! you precious wagabond! (rather louder.) Where's your wife, you willin? (louder still; women of this class are always sympathetic, and work themselves into a tremendous passion on the shortest notice.) Your poor dear wife as you uses worser nor a dog – strike a woman – you a man! (very shrill;) I wish I had you – I'd murder you, I would, if I died for it!' – 'Now be civil,' retorts the man fiercely. 'Be civil, you wiper!' ejaculates the woman contemptuously. 'Ain't it shocking?' she continues, turning round, and appealing to an old woman who is peeping out of one of the little closets we have before described, and who has not the slightest objection to join in the attack, possessing, as she does, the comfortable conviction that she is bolted in. 'Ain't it shocking, ma'am? (Dreadful! says the old woman in a parenthesis, not exactly knowing what the question refers to.) He's got a wife, ma'am, as takes in mangling, and is as 'dustrious and hard-working a young 'ooman as can be, (very fast) as lives in the back parlour of our 'ous, which my husband and me lives in the front one (with great rapidity) – and we hears him a beaten' on her sometimes when he comes home drunk, the whole night through, and not only a beaten' her, but beaten' his own child too, to make her more miserable – ugh, you beast! and she, poor creater, won't swear the peace agin him, nor do nothin', because she likes the wretch arter all – worse luck!' Here, as the woman has completely run herself out of breath, the pawnbroker himself, who has just appeared behind the counter in a gray dressing-gown, embraces the favourable opportunity of putting in a word:– 'Now I won't have none of this sort of thing on my premises!' he interposes with an air of authority. 'Mrs. Mackin, keep yourself to yourself, or you don't get fourpence for a flat iron here; and Jinkins, you leave your ticket here till you're sober, and send your wife for them two planes, for I won't have you in my shop at no price; so make yourself scarce, before I make you scarcer.'

This eloquent address produces anything but the effect desired; the women rail in concert; the man hits about him in all directions, and is in the act of establishing an indisputable claim to gratuitous lodgings for the night, when the entrance of his wife, a wretched, worn-out woman, apparently in the last stage of consumption, whose face bears evident marks of recent ill-usage, and whose strength seems hardly equal to the burden – light enough, God knows! – of the thin, sickly child she carries in her arms, turns his cowardly rage in a safer direction. 'Come home, dear,' cries the miserable creature, in an imploring tone;

'*do* come home, there's a good fellow, and go to bed.' – 'Go home yourself,' rejoins the furious ruffian. 'Do come home quietly,' repeats the wife, bursting into tears. 'Go home yourself,' retorts the husband again, enforcing his argument by a blow which sends the poor creature flying out of the shop. Her 'natural protector' follows her up the court, alternately venting his rage in accelerating her progress, and in knocking the little scanty blue bonnet of the unfortunate child over its still more scanty and faded-looking face.

In the last box, which is situated in the darkest and most obscure corner of the shop, considerably removed from either of the gas-lights, are a young delicate girl of about twenty, and an elderly female, evidently her mother from the resemblance between them, who stand at some distance back, as if to avoid the observation even of the shopman. It is not their first visit to a pawnbroker's shop, for they answer without a moment's hesitation the usual questions, put in a rather respectful manner, and in a much lower tone than usual, of 'What name shall I say? – Your own property, of course? – Where do you live? – Housekeeper or lodger?' They bargain, too, for a higher loan than the shopman is at first inclined to offer, which a perfect stranger would be little disposed to do; and the elder female urges her daughter on, in scarcely audible whispers, to exert her utmost powers of persuasion to obtain an advance of the sum, and expatiate on the value of the articles they have brought to raise a present supply upon. They are a small gold chain and a 'Forget-me-not' ring: the girl's property, for they are both too small for the mother; given her in better times; prized, perhaps, once, for the giver's sake, but parted with now without a struggle; for want has hardened the mother, and her example has hardened the girl, and the prospect of receiving money, coupled with a recollection of the misery they have both endured from the want of it – the coldness of old friends – the stern refusal of some, and the still more galling compassion of others – appears to have obliterated the consciousness of self-humiliation, which the idea of their present situation would once have aroused.

In the next box, is a young female, whose attire, miserably poor, but extremely gaudy, wretchedly cold, but extravagantly fine, too plainly bespeaks her station. The rich satin gown with its faded trimmings, the worn-out thin shoes, and pink silk stockings, the summer bonnet in winter, and the sunken face, where a daub of rouge only serves as an index to the ravages of squandered health never to be regained, and lost happiness never to be restored, and where the practised smile is a wretched mockery of the misery of the heart, cannot be mistaken. There is something in the glimpse she has just caught of her young neighbour, and in the sight of the little trinkets she has offered in pawn, that seems to have awakened in this woman's mind some slumbering recollection, and to have changed, for an instant, her whole demeanour. Her first hasty impulse was to bend forward as if to scan more minutely the appearance of her half-concealed companions; her next, on seeing them involuntarily shrink from her, to retreat to the back of the box, cover her face with her hands, and burst into tears.

There are strange chords in the human heart, which will lie dormant through years of depravity and wickedness, but which will vibrate at last to some slight circumstance apparently trivial in itself, but connected by some undefined and indistinct association, with past days that can never be recalled, and with bitter recollections from which the most degraded creature in existence cannot escape.

There has been another spectator, in the person of a woman in the common shop; the lowest of the low; dirty, unbonneted, flaunting, and slovenly. Her curiosity was at first attracted by the little she could see of the group; then her attention. The half-intoxicated leer changed to an expression of something like interest, and a feeling similar to that we have described, appeared for a moment, and only a moment, to extend itself even to her bosom.

Who shall say how soon these women may change places? The last has but two more stages – the hospital and the grave. How many females situated as her two companions are, and as she may have been once, have terminated the same wretched course, in the same wretched manner! One is already tracing her footsteps with frightful rapidity. How soon may the other follow her example! How many have done the same!

Shabby-genteel People

Shabby-genteel People

There are certain descriptions of people who, oddly enough, appear to appertain exclusively to the metropolis. You meet them, every day, in the streets of London, but no one ever encounters them elsewhere; they seem indigenous to the soil, and to belong as exclusively to London as its own smoke, or the dingy bricks and mortar. We could illustrate the remark by a variety of examples, but in our present sketch, we will only advert to one class as a specimen – that class which is so aptly and expressively designated as 'shabby-genteel.'

Now, shabby people, God knows, may be found anywhere, and genteel people are not articles of greater scarcity out of London than in it, but this compound of the two – this shabby-gentility – is as purely local as the statue at Charing-cross, or the pump at Aldgate. It is worthy of remark, too, that only men are shabby-genteel; a woman is either dirty or slovenly in the extreme, or neat and respectable, however poverty-stricken in appearance. A very poor man, 'who has seen better days,' as the phrase goes, is a strange compound of dirty slovenliness and wretched attempts at a kind of faded smartness.

We will endeavour to explain our conception of the term which forms the title of this paper. If you meet a man, lounging up Drury-lane, or leaning with his back against a post in Long-acre, with his hands in the pockets of a pair of drab trousers plentifully besprinkled with grease-spots; the trousers made very full over the boots, and ornamented with two cords down the outside of each leg – wearing, also, what has been a brown coat with bright buttons, and a hat very much pinched up at the sides cocked over his right eye, do not pity him. He is not shabby-genteel. The 'harmonic meetings' at some fourth-rate public-house, or the purlieus of a private theatre are his chosen haunts; he entertains a rooted antipathy to any kind of work, and is on familiar terms with several pantomime men at the large houses. But, if you see hurrying along a by-street, keeping as close as he can to the area-railings, a man of about forty or fifty, clad in an old rusty suit of threadbare black cloth which shines with constant wear as if it had been bees-waxed, the trousers tightly strapped down, partly for the look of the thing and partly to keep his old shoes from slipping off at the heels – if you observe, too, that his yellowish-white neckerchief is carefully pinned up, to conceal the tattered garment underneath, and that his hands are encased in the remains of an old pair of leather gloves, you may set him down as a shabby-genteel man. A glance at that depressed face, and timorous air of conscious poverty, will make your heart ache – always supposing that you are neither a philosopher nor a political economist.

We were once haunted by a shabby-genteel man; he was bodily present to our senses all day, and he was in our mind's eye all night. The man of whom Sir Walter Scott speaks in his Demonology, did not suffer half the persecution from his imaginary gentleman-usher in black velvet that we sustained from our quondam black cloth.[12] He first attracted our notice, by sitting opposite to us in the reading-room of the British Museum; and what made the man more remarkable was, that he always had before him a couple of shabby-genteel books – two old dogs-eared folios, in mouldy worm-eaten covers, which had once been smart. He was in his chair every morning just as the clock struck ten; he was always the last to leave the room in the afternoon, and when he did, he quitted it with the air of a man who knew not where else to go for warmth and quiet. There he used to sit all day, as close to the table as possible, in order to conceal the lack of buttons on his coat, with his old hat carefully deposited at his feet, where he evidently flattered himself it escaped observation.

About two o'clock, you would see him munching a French roll or a penny loaf; not taking it boldly out of his pocket at once, like a man who knew he was only making a lunch; but breaking off little bits in his pocket, and eating them by stealth. He knew too well it was his dinner.

When we first saw this poor object, we thought it quite impossible that his attire could ever become worse. We even went so far as to speculate on the possibility of his shortly appearing in a decent second-hand suit. We knew nothing about the matter; he grew more and more shabby-genteel every day. The buttons dropped off his waistcoat one by one; then he buttoned his coat; and when one side of the coat was reduced to the same condition as the waistcoat, he buttoned it over on the other side. He looked somewhat better at the beginning of the week than at the conclusion, because the neckerchief, though yellow, was not quite so dingy, and, in the midst of all this wretchedness, he never appeared without gloves and straps. He remained in this state for a week or two. At length, one of the buttons on the back of the coat fell off, and then the man himself disappeared, and we thought he was dead.

We were sitting at the same table about a week after his disappearance, and as our eyes rested on his vacant chair, we insensibly fell into a train of meditation on the subject of his retirement from public life. We were wondering whether he had hung himself, or thrown himself off a bridge, whether he really was dead or had only been arrested, when our conjectures were suddenly set at rest by the entry of the man himself. He had undergone some strange metamorphosis, and walked up the centre of the room with an air which showed he was fully conscious of the improvement in his appearance. It was very odd; his clothes were a fine, deep, glossy black; and yet they looked like the same suit – nay, there were the very darns with which old acquaintance had made us familiar. The hat, too, nobody could mistake the shape of that hat, with its high crown gradually increasing in circumference towards the top. Long service had imparted to it a reddish-brown tint; but, now, it was as black as the coat. The truth flashed suddenly upon us – they had been 'revived.' It is a deceitful liquid that black and blue reviver; we have watched its effects on many a shabby-genteel man. It betrays its victims into a temporary assumption of importance: possibly into the purchase of a new pair of gloves, or a cheap stock, or some other trifling article of dress. It elevates their spirits for a week, only to depress them, if possible, below their original level. It was so in this case; the transient dignity of the unhappy man decreased, in exact proportion as the 'reviver' wore off. The knees of the unmentionables, and the elbows of the coat, and the seams generally soon began to get alarmingly white. The hat was once more deposited under the table, and its owner crept into his seat as quietly as ever.

There was a week of incessant small rain and mist. At its expiration the reviver had entirely vanished, and the shabby-genteel man never afterwards attempted to effect any improvement in his outward appearance.

It would be difficult to name any particular part of town as the principal resort of shabby-genteel men. We have met a great many persons of this description in the Inns of Court. They may be met with, in Holborn between eight and ten any morning, and whoever has the curiosity to enter the Insolvent Debtors' Court will observe both among spectators and practitioners a great variety of them. We never went on 'Change, by any chance, without seeing some shabby-genteel men, and we have often wondered what earthly business they can have there. They will sit there for hours leaning on great, dropsical, mildewed umbrellas, or eating Abernethy biscuits; nobody speaks to them, nor they to any one. On consideration, we remember to have occasionally seen two shabby-genteel men conversing together on 'Change, but our experience assures us that this is an uncommon circumstance, occasioned by the offer of a pinch of snuff, or some such ordinary civility.

It would be a task of equal difficulty, either to assign any particular spot for the residence of these beings, or to endeavour to enumerate their general occupations. We were never engaged in business with more than one shabby-genteel man: he was a drunken engraver, and lived in a damp back-parlour in a new row of houses at Camden-town, half street, half brick-field, somewhere near the canal. A shabby-genteel man may have no occupation, or he may be a corn agent or a coal agent, or a wine-agent, or a collector of debts, or a broker's assistant, or a broken-down attorney. He may be a clerk of the lowest description, or a contributor to the press of the same grade. Whether our readers have noticed these men in their walks as often as we have we know not; this we know – that the miserably poor man (no matter whether he owes his distresses to his own conduct or that of others) who feels his poverty and vainly strives to conceal it, is one of the most pitiable objects in human nature. Such objects, with few exceptions, are shabby-genteel people.

A Walk in a Workhouse

A few Sundays ago, I formed one of the congregation assembled in the chapel of a large metropolitan Workhouse. With the exception of the clergyman and clerk, and a very few officials, there were none but paupers present. The children sat in the galleries; the women in the body of the chapel, and in one of the side aisles; the men in the remaining aisle. The service was decorously performed, though the sermon might have been much better adapted to the comprehension and to the circumstances of the hearers. The usual supplications were offered, with more than the usual significancy in such a place, for the fatherless children and widows, for all sick persons and young children, for all that were desolate and oppressed, for the comforting and helping of the weak-hearted, for the raising-up of them that had fallen; for all that were in danger, necessity, and tribulation. The prayers of the congregation were desired 'for several persons in the various wards, dangerously ill'; and others who were recovering returned their thanks to Heaven.

Among this congregation were some evil-looking young women, and beetle-browed young men; but not many – perhaps that kind of characters kept away. Generally, the faces (those of the children excepted) were depressed and subdued, and wanted colour. Aged people were there, in every variety. Mumbling, blear-eyed, spectacled, stupid, deaf, lame; vacantly winking in the gleams of sun that now and then crept in through the open doors, from the paved yard; shading their listening ears or blinking eyes with their withered hands; poring over their books, leering at nothing, going to sleep, crouching and drooping in corners. There were weird old women, all skeleton within, all bonnet and cloak without, continually wiping their eyes with dirty dusters of pocket-handkerchiefs; and there were ugly old crones, both male and female, with a ghastly kind of contentment upon them which was not at all comforting to see. Upon the whole, it was the dragon, Pauperism, in a very weak and impotent condition; toothless, fangless, drawing his breath heavily enough, and hardly worth chaining up.

When the service was over, I walked with the humane and conscientious gentleman whose duty it was to take that walk, that Sunday morning, through the little world of poverty enclosed within the workhouse walls. It was inhabited by a population of some fifteen hundred or two thousand paupers, ranging from the infant newly born or not yet come into the pauper world to the old man dying on his bed.

In a room opening from a squalid yard, where a number of listless women were lounging to and fro, trying to get warm in the ineffectual sunshine of the tardy May morning, – in the 'Itch Ward,' not to compromise the truth, – a woman, such as Hogarth has often drawn, was hurriedly getting on her gown before a dusty fire.[13] She was the nurse, or wardswoman, of that insalubrious department – herself a pauper – flabby, raw-boned, untidy – unpromising and coarse of aspect as need be. But on being spoken to about the patients whom she had in charge, she turned round, with her shabby gown half on, half off, and fell a crying with all her might. Not for show, not querulously, not in any mawkish sentiment, but in the deep grief and affliction of her heart; turning away her dishevelled head; sobbing most bitterly, wringing her hands, and letting fall abundance of great tears, that choked her utterance. What was the matter with the nurse of the itch-ward? Oh, 'the dropped child' was dead! Oh, the child that was found in the street, and she had brought up ever since, had died an hour ago, and see where the little creature lay, beneath this cloth! The dear, the pretty dear!

The dropped child seemed too small and poor a thing for Death to be in earnest with, but Death had taken it; and already its diminutive form was neatly washed, composed, and stretched as if in sleep upon a box. I thought I heard a voice from Heaven saying, It shall be well for thee, O nurse of the itch-ward, when some less gentle pauper does those offices to thy cold form, that such as the dropped child are the angels who behold my Father's face!

In another room were several ugly old women crouching, witch-like, round a hearth, and chattering and nodding, after the manner of the monkeys. 'All well here? And enough to eat?' A general chattering and chuckling; at last an answer from a volunteer. 'Oh, yes, gentleman! Bless you gentleman! Lord bless the parish of St. So-and-So! It feed the hungry, Sir, and give drink to the thusty, and it warm them which is cold, so it do, and good luck to the parish of St. So-and-So, and thankee gentleman!' Elsewhere, a party of pauper nurses were at dinner. 'How do *you* get on?' 'Oh, pretty well, sir! We works hard, and we lives hard – like the sodgers!'[14]

In another room, a kind of purgatory or place of transition, six or eight noisy madwomen were gathered together, under the superintendence of one sane attendant. Among them was a girl of two or three and twenty, very prettily dressed, of most respectable appearance, and good manners, who had been brought in from the house where she had lived as domestic servant (having, I suppose, no friends), on account of being subject to epileptic fits, and requiring to be removed under the influence of a very bad one. She was by no means of the same stuff, or the same breeding, or the same experience, or in the same state of mind, as those by whom she was surrounded; and she pathetically complained that the daily association and the nightly noise made her worse, and was driving her mad – which was perfectly evident. The case was noted for enquiry and redress, but she said she had already been there for some weeks.

If this girl had stolen her mistress's watch, I do not hesitate to say she would, in all probability, have been infinitely better off. Bearing in mind, in the present brief description of this walk, not only the facts already stated in this Journal, in reference to the Model Prison at Pentonville, but the general treatment of convicted prisoners under the associated silent system too, it must be once more distinctly set before the reader, that we have come to this absurd, this dangerous, this monstrous pass, that the dishonest felon is, in respect of cleanliness, order, diet, and accommodation, better provided for, and taken care of, than the honest pauper.

And this conveys no special imputation on the workhouse of the parish of St. So-and-So, where, on the contrary, I saw many things to commend. It was very agreeable, recollecting that most infamous and atrocious enormity committed at Tooting, – an enormity which, a hundred years hence, will still be vividly remembered in the byways of English life, and which has done more to engender a gloomy discontent and suspicion among many thousands of the people than all the Chartist leaders could have done in all their lives, – to find the pauper children in this workhouse looking robust and well, and apparently the objects of very great care. In the Infant School – a large, light, airy room at the top of the building – the little creatures, being at dinner, and eating their potatoes heartily, were not cowed by the presence of strange visitors, but stretched out their small hands to be shaken, with a very pleasant confidence. And it was comfortable to see two mangy pauper rocking-horses rampant in a corner. In the girls' school, where the dinner was also in progress, everything bore a cheerful and healthy aspect. The meal was over in the boys' school, by the time of our arrival there and the room was not yet quite rearranged; but the boys were roaming unrestrained about a large and airy yard, as any other schoolboys might have done. Some of them had been drawing large ships upon the schoolroom wall; and if they had a mast with shrouds and stays set up for practice (as they have in the Middlesex House of Correction), it would be so much the better. At present, if a boy should feel a strong impulse upon him to learn the art of going aloft, he could only gratify it, I presume, as the men and women paupers gratify their aspirations after better board and lodging, by smashing as many workhouse windows as possible, and being promoted to prison.

In one place, the Newgate of the Workhouse,[15] a company of boys and youths were locked up in a yard alone; their day-room being a kind of kennel where the casual poor used formerly to be littered down at night. Divers of them had been there some long time. 'Are they never going away?' was the natural enquiry. 'Most of them are crippled, in some form or other,' said the Wardsman, 'and not fit for anything.' They slunk about, like dispirited wolves or hyaenas; and made a pounce at their food when it was served out, much as those animals do. The big-headed idiot shuffling his feet along the pavement, in the sunlight outside, was a more agreeable object every way.

Groves of babies in arms; groves of mothers and other sick women in bed; groves of lunatics; jungles of men in stone-paved down-stairs day-rooms, waiting for their dinners; longer and longer groves of old people, in up-stairs Infirmary wards, wearing out life, God knows how – this was the scenery through which the walk lay, for two hours. In some of these latter chambers there were pictures stuck against the wall, and a neat display of crockery and pewter on a kind of sideboard; now and then it was a treat to see a plant or two; in almost every ward there was a cat.

In all of these Long Walks of aged and infirm, some old people were bed-ridden, and had been for a long time; some were sitting on their beds half naked; some dying in their beds; some out of bed, and sitting at a table near the fire. A sullen or lethargic indifference to what was asked, a blunted sensibility to everything but warmth and food, a moody absence of complaint as being of no use, a dogged silence and resentful desire to be left alone again, I thought were generally apparent. On our walking into the midst of one of these dreary perspectives of old men, nearly the following little dialogue took place, the nurse not being immediately at hand:

'All well here?'

No answer. An old man in a Scotch cap sitting among others on a form at the table, eating out of a tin porringer, pushes back his cap a little to look at us, claps it down on his forehead again with the palm of his hand, and goes on eating.

'All well here?' (repeated).

No answer. Another old man sitting on his bed, paralytically peeling a boiled potato, lifts his head, and stares.

'Enough to eat?'

No answer. Another old man, in bed, turns himself and coughs.

'How are *you* today?' To the last old man.

That old man says nothing; but another old man, a tall old man of very good address, speaking with perfect correctness, comes forward from somewhere, and volunteers an answer. The reply almost always proceeds from a volunteer, and not from the person looked at or spoken to.

'We are very old, sir,' in a mild, distinct voice. 'We can't expect to be well, most of us.'

'Are you comfortable?'

'I have no complaint to make, Sir.' With a half shake of his head, a half shrug of his shoulders, and a kind of apologetic smile.

'Enough to eat?'

'Why, Sir, I have but a poor appetite,' with the same air as before; 'and yet I get through my allowance very easily.'

'But,' showing a porringer with a Sunday dinner in it, 'here is a portion of mutton and three potatoes. You can't starve on that?'[16]

'Oh, dear, no, Sir,' with the same apologetic air. 'Not starve.'

'What do you want?'

'We have very little bread, sir. It's an exceedingly small quantity of bread.'

The nurse, who is now rubbing her hands at the questioner's elbow, interferes with, 'It ain't much raly, sir. You see they've only six ounces a day, and when they've took their breakfast, there *can* only be a little left for night, sir.'

Another old man, hitherto invisible, rises out of his bedclothes, as out of a grave, and looks on.

'You have tea at night?' The questioner is still addressing the well-spoken old man.

'Yes, Sir, we have tea at night.'

'And you save what bread you can from the morning, to eat with it?'

'Yes, Sir – if we can save any.'

'And you want more to eat with it?'

'Yes, sir.' With a very anxious face.

The questioner, in the kindness of his heart, appears a little discomposed, and changes the subject.

'What has become of the old man who used to lie in that bed in the corner?'

The nurse don't remember what old man is referred to. There has been such a many old men. The well-spoken old man is doubtful. The spectral old man who has come to life in bed says, 'Billy Stevens.' Another old man who has previously had his head in the fireplace pipes out,

'Charley Walters.'

Something like a feeble interest is awakened. I suppose Charley Walters had conversation in him.

'He's dead!' says the piping old man.

Another old man, with one eye screwed up, hastily displaces the piping old man, and says:

'Yes! Charley Walters died in that bed, and – and –'

'Billy Stevens,' persists the spectral old man.

'No, no! and Johnny Rogers died in that bed, and – and – they're both on 'em dead – and Sam'l Bowyer;' (this seems very extraordinary to him), 'he went out!'

With this he subsides, and all the old men (having had quite enough of it) subside, and the spectral old man goes into his grave again, and takes the shade of Billy Stevens with him.

As we turn to go out at the door, another previously invisible old man, a hoarse old man in a flannel gown, is standing there, as if he had just come up through the floor.

'I beg your pardon, Sir, could I take the liberty of saying a word?'

'Yes; what is it?'

'I am greatly better in my health, Sir; but what I want to get me quite round,' with his hand on his throat, 'is a little fresh air, sir. It has always done my complaint so much good, Sir. The regular leave for going out comes round so seldom, that if the gentlemen, next Friday, would give me leave to go out walking, now and then – for only an hour or so, sir! –'

Who could wonder, looking through those weary vistas of bed and infirmity, that it should do him good to meet with some other scenes, and assure himself that there was something else on earth? Who could help wondering why the old men lived on as they did; what grasp they had on life; what crumbs of interest or occupation they could pick up from its bare board; whether Charley Walters had ever described to them the days when he kept company with some old pauper woman in the bud, or Billy Stevens ever told them of the time when he was a dweller in the far-off foreign land called Home!

The morsel of burnt child, lying in another room, so patiently, in bed, wrapped in lint, and looking steadfastly at us with his bright quiet eyes when we spoke to him kindly, looked as if the knowledge of these things, and of all the tender things there are to think about, might have been in his mind – as if he thought, with us, that there was a fellow-feeling in the pauper nurses which appeared to make them more kind to their charges than the race of common nurses in the hospitals – as if he mused upon the future of some older children lying around him in the same place, and thought it best, perhaps, all things considered, that he should die – as if he knew, without fear, of those ma ny coffins, made and unmade, piled up in the store below, and of his unknown friend, 'the dropped child,' calm upon the box-lid covered with a cloth. But there was something wistful and appealing, too, in his tiny face, as if, in the midst of all the hard necessities and incongruities he pondered on, he pleaded, in behalf of the helpless and the aged poor, for a little more liberty – and a little more bread.

Tramps

The chance use of the word 'Tramp' in my last paper, brought that numerous fraternity so vividly before my mind's eye, that I had no sooner laid down my pen than a compulsion was upon me to take it up again, and make notes of the tramps whom I perceived on all the summer roads in all directions.[17]

Whenever a tramp sits down to rest by the wayside, he sits with his legs in a dry ditch; and whenever he goes to sleep (which is very often indeed), he goes to sleep on his back. Yonder, by the high road, glaring white in the bright sunshine, lies, on the dusty bit of turf under the bramble-bush that fences the coppice from the highway, the tramp of the order savage, fast asleep. He lies on the broad of his back, with his face turned up to the sky, and one of his ragged arms loosely thrown across his face. His bundle (what can be the contents of that mysterious bundle, to make it worth his while to carry it about?) is thrown down beside him, and the waking woman with him sits with her legs in the ditch, and her back to the road. She wears her bonnet rakishly perched on the front of her head, to shade her face from the sun in walking, and she ties her skirts round her in conventionally tight tramp-fashion with a sort of apron. You can seldom catch sight of her, resting thus, without seeing her in a despondently defiant manner doing something to her hair or her bonnet, and glancing at you between her fingers. She does not often go to sleep herself in the daytime, but will sit for any length of time beside the man. And his slumberous propensities would not seem to be referable to the fatigue of carrying the bundle, for she carries it much oftener and further than he. When they are afoot, you will mostly find him slouching on ahead, in a gruff temper, while she lags heavily behind with the burden. He is given to personally correcting her, too – which phase of his character develops itself oftenest, on benches outside alehouse doors – and she appears to become strongly attached to him for these reasons; it may usually be noticed that when the poor creature has a bruised face, she is the most affectionate. He has no occupation whatever, this order of tramp, and has no object whatever in going anywhere. He will sometimes call himself a brickmaker, or a sawyer, but only when he takes an imaginary flight. He generally represents himself, in a vague way, as looking out for a job of work; but he never did work, he never does, and he never will. It is a favourite fiction with him, however (as if he were the most industrious character on earth), that *you* never work; and as he goes past your garden and sees you looking at your flowers, you will overhear him growl with a strong sense of contrast, '*You* are a lucky hidle devil, *you* are!'

The slinking tramp is of the same hopeless order, and has the same injured conviction on him that you were born to whatever you possess, and never did anything to get it: but he is of a less audacious disposition. He will stop before your gate, and say to his female companion with an air of constitutional humility and propitiation – to edify any one who may be within hearing behind a blind or a bush – 'This is a sweet spot, ain't it? A lovelly spot! And I wonder if they'd give two poor footsore travellers like me and you, a drop of fresh water out of such a pretty genteel crib? We'd take it wery koind on 'em, wouldn't us? Wery koind, upon my word, us would?' He has a quick sense of a dog in the vicinity, and will extend his modestly-injured propitiation to the dog chained up in your yard; remarking, as he slinks at the yard gate, 'Ah! You are a foine breed o' dog, too, and *you* ain't kep for nothink! I'd take it wery koind o' your master if he'd elp a traveller and his woife as envies no gentlefolk their good fortun, wi' a bit o' your broken wittles. He'd never know the want of it, nor more would you. Don't bark like that, at poor persons as never done you no arm; the poor is down-trodden and broke enough without that; O DON'T!' He generally heaves a prodigious sigh in moving away, and always looks up the lane and down the lane, and up the road and down the road, before going on.

Both of these orders of tramp are of a very robust habit; let the hard-working labourer at whose cottage-door they prowl and beg, have the ague never so badly, these tramps are sure to be in good health.

There is another kind of tramp, whom you encounter this bright summer day – say, on a road with the sea-breeze making its dust lively, and sails of ships in the blue distance beyond the slope of Down. As you walk enjoyingly on, you descry in the perspective at the bottom of a steep hill up which your way lies, a figure that appears to be sitting airily on a gate, whistling in a cheerful and disengaged manner. As you approach nearer to it, you observe the figure to slide down from the gate, to desist from whistling, to uncock its hat, to become tender of foot, to depress its head and elevate its shoulders, and to present all the characteristics of profound despondency. Arriving at the bottom of the hill and coming close to the figure, you observe it to be the figure of a shabby young man. He is moving painfully forward, in the direction in which you are going, and his mind is so preoccupied with his misfortunes that he is not aware of your approach until you are close upon him at the hill-foot. When he is aware of you, you discover him to be a remarkably well-behaved young man, and a remarkably well-spoken young man. You know him to be well-behaved, by his respectful manner of touching his hat; you know him to be well-spoken, by his smooth manner of expressing himself. He says in a flowing confidential voice, and without punctuation, 'I ask your pardon sir but if you would excuse the liberty of being so addressed upon the public Iway by one who is almost reduced to rags though it as not always been so and by no fault of his own but through ill elth in his family and many unmerited sufferings it would be a great obligation sir to know the time.' You give the well-spoken young man the time. The well-spoken young man, keeping well up with you, resumes: 'I am aware sir that it is a liberty to intrude a further question on a gentleman walking for his entertainment but might I make so bold as ask the favour of the way to Dover sir and about the distance?' You inform the well-spoken young man that the way to Dover is straight on, and the distance some eighteen miles. The well-spoken young man becomes greatly agitated. 'In the condition to which I am reduced,' says he, 'I could not ope to reach Dover before dark even if my shoes were in a state to take me there or my feet were in a state to old out over the flinty road and were not on the bare ground of which any gentleman has the means to satisfy himself by looking. Sir may I take the liberty of speaking to you?' As the well-spoken young man keeps so well up with you that you can't prevent his taking the liberty of speaking to you, he goes on, with fluency: 'Sir it is not begging that is my intention for I was brought up by the best of mothers and begging is not my trade I should not know sir how to follow it as a trade if such were my shameful wishes for the best of mothers long taught otherwise and in the best of omes though now reduced to take the present liberty on the Iway Sir my business was the law-stationering and I was favourably known to the Solicitor-General the Attorney-General the majority of the Judges and the ole of the legal profession but through ill elth in my family and the treachery of a friend for whom I became security and he no other than my own wife's brother the brother of my own wife I was cast forth with my tender partner and three young children not to beg for I will sooner die of deprivation but to make my way to the sea-port town of Dover where I have a relative in respect not only that will assist me but that would trust me with untold gold Sir in appier times and hare this calamity fell upon me I made for my amusement when I little thought that I should ever need it excepting for my air this' – here the well-spoken young man put his hand into his breast – 'this comb! Sir I implore you in the name of charity to purchase a tortoiseshell comb which is a genuine article at any price that your humanity may put upon it and may the blessings of a ouseless family awaiting with beating arts the return of a husband and a father from Dover upon the cold stone seats of London-bridge ever attend you Sir may I take the liberty of speaking to you I implore you to buy this comb!' By this time, being a reasonably good walker, you will have been too much for the well-spoken young man, who will stop short and express his disgust and his want of breath, in a long expectoration, as you leave him behind.

Towards the end of the same walk, on the same bright summer day, at the corner of the next little town or village, you may find another kind of tramp, embodied in the persons of a most exemplary couple whose only improvidence appears to have been, that they spent the last of their little All on soap. They are a man and woman, spotless to behold – John Anderson, with the frost on his short smock-frock instead of his 'pow,'[18] attended by Mrs. Anderson. John is over-ostentatious of the frost upon his raiment, and wears a curious and, you would say, an almost unnecessary demonstration of girdle of white linen wound about his waist – a girdle, snowy as Mrs. Anderson's apron. This cleanliness was the expiring effort of the respectable couple, and nothing then remained to Mr. Anderson but to get chalked upon his spade in snow-white copy-book characters, HUNGRY! and to sit down here. Yes; one thing more remained to Mr. Anderson – his character; Monarchs could not deprive him of his hard-earned character. Accordingly, as you come up with this spectacle of virtue in distress, Mrs. Anderson rises, and with a decent curtsey presents for your consideration a certificate from a Doctor of Divinity, the reverend the Vicar of Upper Dodgington, who informs his Christian friends and all whom it may concern that the bearers, John Anderson and lawful wife, are persons to whom you cannot be too liberal. This benevolent pastor omitted no work of his hands to fit the good couple out, for with half an eye you can recognise his autograph on the spade.

Another class of tramp is a man, the most valuable part of whose stock-in-trade is a highly perplexed demeanour. He is got up like a countryman, and you will often come upon the poor fellow, while he is endeavouring to decipher the inscription on a milestone – quite a fruitless endeavour, for he cannot read. He asks your pardon, he truly does (he is very slow of speech, this tramp, and he looks in a bewildered way all round the prospect while he talks to you), but all of us shold do as we wold be done by, and he'll take it kind, if you'll put a power man in the right road fur to jine his eldest son as has broke his leg bad in the masoning, and is in this heere Orspit'l as is wrote down by Squire Pouncerby's own hand as wold not tell a lie fur no man. He then produces from under his dark frock (being always very slow and perplexed) a neat but worn old leathern purse, from which he takes a scrap of paper. On this scrap of paper is written, by Squire Pouncerby, of The Grove, 'Please to direct the Bearer, a poor but very worthy man, to the Sussex County Hospital, near Brighton' – a matter of some difficulty at the moment, seeing that the request comes suddenly upon you in the depths of Hertfordshire. The more you endeavour to indicate where Brighton is – when you have with the greatest difficulty remembered – the less the devoted father can be made to comprehend, and the more obtusely he stares at the prospect; whereby, being reduced to extremity, you recommend the faithful parent to begin by going to St. Albans, and present him with half-a-crown. It does him good, no doubt, but scarcely helps him forward, since you find him lying drunk that same evening in the wheelwright's sawpit under the shed where the felled trees are, opposite the sign of the Three Jolly Hedgers.

But, the most vicious, by far, of all the idle tramps, is the tramp who pretends to have been a gentleman. 'Educated,' he writes, from the village beer-shop in pale ink of a ferruginous complexion; 'educated at Trin. Coll. Cam. – nursed in the lap of affluence – once in my small way the pattron of the Muses,' &c. &c. &c. – surely a sympathetic mind will not withhold a trifle, to help him on to the market-town where he thinks of giving a Lecture to the *fruges consumere nati*, on things in general?[19] This shameful creature lolling about hedge tap-rooms in his ragged clothes, now so far from being black that they look as if they never can have been black, is more selfish and insolent than even the savage tramp. He would sponge on the poorest boy for a farthing, and spurn him when he had got it; he would interpose (if he could get anything by it) between the baby and the mother's breast. So much lower than the company he keeps, for his maudlin assumption of being higher, this pitiless rascal blights the summer road as he maunders on between the luxuriant hedges; where (to my thinking) even the wild convolvulus and rose and sweet-briar, are the worse for his going by, and need time to recover from the taint of him in the air.

The young fellows who trudge along barefoot, five or six together, their boots slung over their shoulders, their shabby bundles under their arms, their sticks newly cut from some roadside wood, are not eminently prepossessing, but are much less objectionable. There is a tramp-fellowship among them. They pick one another up at resting stations, and go on in companies. They always go at a fast swing – though they generally limp too – and there is invariably one of the company who has much ado to keep up with the rest. They generally talk about horses, and any other means of locomotion than walking: or, one of the company relates some recent experiences of the road – which are always disputes and difficulties. As for example. 'So as I'm a standing at the pump in the market, blest if there don't come up a Beadle, and he ses, "Mustn't stand here," he ses. "Why not?" I ses. "No beggars allowed in this town," he ses. "Who's a beggar?" I ses. "You are," he ses. "Who ever see *me* beg? Did *you*?" I ses. "Then you're a tramp," he ses. "I'd rather be that than a Beadle," I ses.' (The company express great approval.) '"Would you?" he ses to me. "Yes, I would," I ses to him. "Well," he ses, "anyhow, get out of this town." "Why, blow your little town!" I ses, "who wants to be in it? Wot does your dirty little town mean by comin' and stickin' itself in the road to anywhere? Why don't you get a shovel and a barrer, and clear your town out o' people's way?"' (The company expressing the highest approval and laughing aloud, they all go down the hill.)

Then, there are the tramp handicraft men. Are they not all over England, in this Midsummer time? Where does the lark sing, the corn grow, the mill turn, the river run, and they are not among the lights and shadows, tinkering, chair-mending, umbrella-mending, clock-mending, knife-grinding? Surely, a pleasant thing, if we were in that condition of life, to grind our way through Kent, Sussex, and Surrey. For the first six weeks or so, we should see the sparks we ground off, fiery bright against a background of green wheat and green leaves. A little later, and the ripe harvest would pale our sparks from red to yellow, until we got the dark newly-turned land for a background again, and they were red once more. By that time, we should have ground our way to the sea cliffs, and the whirr of our wheel would be lost in the breaking of the waves. Our next variety in sparks would be derived from contrast with the gorgeous medley of colours in the autumn woods, and, by the time we had ground our way round to the heathy lands between Reigate and Croydon, doing a prosperous stroke of business all along, we should show like a little firework in the light frosty air, and be the next best thing to the blacksmith's forge. Very agreeable, too, to go on a chair-mending tour. What judges we should be of rushes, and how knowingly (with a sheaf and a bottomless chair at our back) we should lounge on bridges, looking over at osier-beds! Among all the innumerable occupations that cannot possibly be transacted without the assistance of lookers-on, chair-mending may take a station in the first rank. When we sat down with our backs against the barn or the public-house, and began to mend, what a sense of popularity would grow upon us! When all the children came to look at us, and the tailor, and the general dealer, and the farmer who had been giving a small order at the little saddler's, and the groom from the great house, and the publican, and even the two skittle-players (and here note that, howsoever busy all the rest of village human-kind may be, there will always be two people with leisure to play at skittles, wherever village skittles are), what encouragement would be on us to plait and weave! No one looks at us while we plait and weave these words. Clock-mending again. Except for the slight inconvenience of carrying a clock under our arm, and the monotony of making the bell go, whenever we came to a human habitation, what a pleasant privilege to give a voice to the dumb cottage-clock, and set it talking to the cottage family again! Likewise we foresee great interest in going round by the park plantations, under the overhanging boughs (hares, rabbits, partridges, and pheasants, scudding like mad across and across the chequered ground before us), and so over the park ladder, and through the wood, until we came to the Keeper's lodge. Then, would the Keeper be discoverable at his door, in a deep nest of leaves, smoking his pipe. Then, on our accosting him in the way of our trade, would he call to Mrs. Keeper, respecting 't'ould clock' in the kitchen. Then, would Mrs. Keeper ask us into the lodge, and on due examination we should offer to make a good job of it for eighteenpence; which offer, being accepted, would set us tinkling and clinking among the chubby, awe-struck little Keepers for an hour and more. So completely to the family's satisfaction would we achieve our work, that the Keeper would mention how that there was something wrong with the bell of the turret stable-clock up at the Hall, and that if we thought good of going up to the housekeeper on the chance of that job too, why he would take us. Then, should we go, among the branching oaks and the deep fern, by silent ways of mystery known to the Keeper, seeing the herd glancing here and there as we went along, until we came to the old Hall, solemn and grand. Under the Terrace Flower Garden, and round by the stables, would the Keeper take us in, and as we passed we should observe how spacious and stately the stables, and how fine the painting of the horses' names over their stalls, and how solitary all: the family being in London. Then, should we find ourselves presented to the housekeeper, sitting, in hushed state, at needlework, in a bay-window looking out upon a mighty grim red-brick quadrangle, guarded by stone lions disrespectfully throwing somersaults over the escutcheons of the noble family. Then, our services accepted and we insinuated with a candle into the stable-turret, we should find it to be a mere question of pendulum, but one that would hold us until dark. Then, should we fall to work, with a general impression of Ghosts being about, and of pictures indoors that of a certainty came out of their frames and 'walked,' if the family would only own it. Then, should we work and work, until the day gradually turned to dusk, and even until the dusk gradually turned to dark. Our task at length accomplished, we should be taken into an enormous servants' hall, and there regaled with beef and bread, and powerful ale. Then, paid freely, we should be at liberty to go, and should be told by a pointing helper to keep round over yinder by the blasted ash, and so straight through the woods, till we should see the town-lights right afore us. Then, feeling lonesome, should we desire upon the whole, that the ash had not been blasted, or that the helper had had the manners not to mention it. However, we should keep on, all right, until suddenly the stable bell would strike ten in the dolefullest way, quite chilling our blood, though we had so lately taught him how to acquit himself. Then, as we went on, should we recall old stories, and dimly consider what it would be most advisable to do, in the event of a tall figure, all in white, with saucer eyes, coming up and saying, 'I want you to come to a churchyard and mend a church clock. Follow me!' Then, should we make a burst to get clear of the trees, and should soon find ourselves in the open, with the town-lights bright ahead of us. So should we lie that night at the ancient sign of the Crispin and Crispanus, and rise early next morning to be betimes on tramp again.[20]

Bricklayers often tramp, in twos and threes, lying by night at their 'lodges,' which are scattered all over the country. Bricklaying is another of the occupations that can by no means be transacted in rural parts, without the assistance of spectators – of as many as can be convened. In thinly-peopled spots, I have known brick-layers on tramp, coming up with bricklayers at work, to be so sensible of the indispensability of lookers-on, that they themselves have sat up in that capacity, and have been unable to subside into the acceptance of a proffered share in the job, for two or three days together. Sometimes, the 'navvy,' on tramp, with an extra pair of half-boots over his shoulder, a bag, a bottle, and a can, will take a similar part in a job of excavation, and will look at it without engaging in it, until all his money is gone. The current of my uncommercial pursuits caused me only last summer to want a little body of workmen for a certain spell of work in a pleasant part of the country; and I was at one time honoured with the attendance of as many as seven-and-twenty, who were looking at six.

Who can be familiar with any rustic highway in summer-time, without storing up knowledge of the many tramps who go from one oasis of town or village to another, to sell a stock in trade, apparently not worth a shilling when sold? Shrimps are a favourite commodity for this kind of speculation, and so are cakes of a soft and spongy character, coupled with Spanish nuts and brandy balls. The stock is carried on the head in a basket, and, between the head and the basket, are the trestles on which the stock is displayed at trading times. Fleet of foot, but a care-worn class of tramp this, mostly; with a certain stiffness of neck, occasioned by much anxious balancing of baskets; and also with a long, Chinese sort of eye, which an overweighted forehead would seem to have squeezed into that form.

On the hot dusty roads near seaport towns and great rivers, behold the tramping Soldier. And if you should happen never to have asked yourself whether his uniform is suited to his work, perhaps the poor fellow's appearance as he comes distressfully towards you, with his absurdly tight jacket unbuttoned, his neck-gear in his hand, and his legs well chafed by his trousers of baize, may suggest the personal inquiry, how you think *you* would like it. Much better the tramping Sailor, although his cloth is somewhat too thick for land service. But, why the tramping merchant-mate should put on a black velvet waistcoat, for a chalky country in the dog-days, is one of the great secrets of nature that will never be discovered.

I have my eye upon a piece of Kentish road, bordered on either side by a wood, and having on one hand, between the road-dust and the trees, a skirting patch of grass. Wild flowers grow in abundance on this spot, and it lies high and airy, with a distant river stealing steadily away to the ocean, like a man's life. To gain the milestone here, which the moss, primroses, violets, blue-bells, and wild roses, would soon render illegible but for peering travellers pushing them aside with their sticks, you must come up a steep hill, come which way you may. So, all the tramps with carts or caravans – the Gipsy-tramp, the Show-tramp, the Cheap Jack[21] – find it impossible to resist the temptations of the place, and all turn the horse loose when they come to it, and boil the pot. Bless the place, I love the ashes of the vagabond fires that have scorched its grass! What tramp children do I see here, attired in a handful of rags, making a gymnasium of the shafts of the cart, making a feather-bed of the flints and brambles, making a toy of the hobbled old horse who is not much more like a horse than any cheap toy would be! Here, do I encounter the cart of mats and brooms and baskets – with all thoughts of business given to the evening wind – with the stew made and being served out – with Cheap Jack and Dear Jill striking soft music out of the plates that are rattled like warlike cymbals when put up for auction at fairs and markets – their minds so influenced (no doubt) by the melody of the nightingales as they begin to sing in the woods behind them, that if I were to propose to deal, they would sell me anything at cost price. On this hallowed ground has it been my happy privilege (let me whisper it), to behold the White-haired Lady with the pink eyes, eating meat-pie with the Giant: while, by the hedge-side, on the box of blankets which I knew contained the snakes, were set forth the cups and saucers and the teapot. It was on an evening in August, that I chanced upon this ravishing spectacle, and I noticed that, whereas the

Giant reclined half concealed beneath the overhanging boughs and seemed indifferent to Nature, the white hair of the gracious Lady streamed free in the breath of evening, and her pink eyes found pleasure in the landscape. I heard only a single sentence of her uttering, yet it bespoke a talent for modest repartee. The ill-mannered Giant – accursed be his evil race! – had interrupted the Lady in some remark, and, as I passed that enchanted corner of the wood, she gently reproved him, with the words, 'Now, Cobby;' – Cobby! so short a name! – 'ain't one fool enough to talk at a time?'

Within appropriate distance of this magic ground, though not so near it as that the song trolled from tap or bench at door, can invade its woodland silence, is a little hostelry which no man possessed of a penny was ever known to pass in warm weather. Before its entrance, are certain pleasant, trimmed limes; likewise, a cool well, with so musical a bucket-handle that its fall upon the bucket rim will make a horse prick up his ears and neigh, upon the droughty road half a mile off. This is a house of great resort for haymaking tramps and harvest tramps, insomuch that as they sit within, drinking their mugs of beer, their relinquished scythes and reaping-hooks glare out of the open windows, as if the whole establishment were a family war-coach of Ancient Britons. Later in the season, the whole country-side, for miles and miles, will swarm with hopping tramps. They come in families, men, women, and children, every family provided with a bundle of bedding, an iron pot, a number of babies, and too often with some poor sick creature quite unfit for the rough life, for whom they suppose the smell of the fresh hop to be a sovereign remedy. Many of these hoppers are Irish, but many come from London. They crowd all the roads, and camp under all the hedges and on all the scraps of common-land, and live among and upon the hops until they are all picked, and the hop-gardens, so beautiful through the summer, look as if they had been laid waste by an invading army. Then, there is a vast exodus of tramps out of the country; and if you ride or drive round any turn of any road, at more than a foot pace, you will be bewildered to find that you have charged into the bosom of fifty families, and that there are splashing up all around you, in the utmost prodigality of confusion, bundles of bedding, babies, iron pots, and a good-humoured multitude of both sexes and all ages, equally divided between perspiration and intoxication.

The Begging-letter Writer

He is a 'Household Word.' We all know something of him. The amount of money he annually diverts from wholesome and useful purposes in the United Kingdom, would be a set-off against the Window Tax. He is one of the most shameless frauds and impositions of this time. In his idleness, his mendacity, and the immeasurable harm he does to the deserving, – dirtying the stream of true benevolence, and muddling the brains of foolish justices, with inability to distinguish between the base coin of distress, and the true currency we have always among us, – he is more worthy of Norfolk Island than three-fourths of the worst characters who are sent there.[22] Under any rational system, he would have been sent there long ago.

I, the writer of this paper, have been, for some time, a chosen receiver of Begging Letters. For fourteen years, my house has been made as regular a Receiving House for such communications as any one of the great branch Post-Offices is for general correspondence. I ought to know something of the Begging-Letter Writer. He has besieged my door at all hours of the day and night; he has fought my servant; he has lain in ambush for me, going out and coming in; he has followed me out of town into the country; he has appeared at provincial hotels, where I have been staying for only a few hours; he has written to me from immense distances, when I have been out of England. He has fallen sick; he has died and been buried; he has come to life again, and again departed from this transitory scene; he has been his own son, his own mother, his own baby, his idiot brother, his uncle, his aunt, his aged grandfather. He has wanted a greatcoat, to go to India in; a pound to set him up in life for ever; a pair of boots to take him to the coast of China; a hat, to get him into a permanent situation under Government. He has frequently been exactly seven-and-sixpence short of independence. He has had such openings at Liverpool – posts of great trust and confidence in merchants' houses, which nothing but seven-and-sixpence was wanting to him to secure – that I wonder he is not Mayor of that flourishing town at the present moment.

The natural phenomena of which he has been the victim, are of a most astounding nature. He has had two children who have never grown up; who have never had anything to cover them at night; who have been continually driving him mad, by asking in vain for food; who have never come out of fevers and measles (which, I suppose, has accounted for his fuming his letters with tobacco smoke, as a disinfectant); who have never changed in the least degree through fourteen long revolving years. As to his wife, what that suffering woman has undergone, nobody knows. She has always been in an interesting situation through the same long period, and has never been confined yet. His devotion to her has been unceasing. He has never cared for himself; *he* could have perished – he would rather, in short – but was it not his Christian duty as a man, a husband, and a father, to write begging letters when he looked at her? (He has usually remarked that he would call in the evening for an answer to this question.)

He has been the sport of the strangest misfortunes. What his brother has done to him would have broken anybody else's heart. His brother went into business with him, and ran away with the money; his brother got him to be security for an immense sum and left him to pay it; his brother would have given him employment to the tune of hundreds a-year, if he would have consented to write letters on a Sunday; his brother enunciated principles incompatible with his religious views, and he could not (in consequence) permit his brother to provide for him. His landlord has never shown a spark of human feeling. When he put in that execution I don't know, but he has never taken it out. The broker's man has grown grey in possession. They will have to bury him some day.

He has been attached to every conceivable pursuit. He has been in the army, in the navy, in the church, in the law;

connected with the press, the fine arts, public institutions, every description and grade of business. He has been brought up as a gentleman; he has been at every college in Oxford and Cambridge; he can quote Latin in his letters (but generally misspells some minor English word); he can tell you what Shakespeare says about begging, better than you know it. It is to be observed, that in the midst of his afflictions he always reads the newspapers; and rounds off his appeal with some allusion, that may be supposed to be in my way, to the popular subject of the hour.

His life presents a series of inconsistencies. Sometimes he has never written such a letter before. He blushes with shame. That is the first time; that shall be the last. Don't answer it, and let it be understood that, then, he will kill himself quietly. Sometimes (and more frequently) he *has* written a few such letters. Then he encloses the answers, with an intimation that they are of inestimable value to him, and a request that they may be carefully returned. He is fond of enclosing something – verses, letters, pawnbrokers' duplicates, anything to necessitate an answer. He is very severe upon 'the pampered minion of fortune,' who refused him the half-sovereign referred to in the enclosure number two – but he knows me better.

He writes in a variety of styles; sometimes in low spirits; sometimes quite jocosely. When he is in low spirits he writes down-hill and repeats words – these little indications being expressive of the perturbation of his mind. When he is more vivacious, he is frank with me; he is quite the agreeable rattle. I know what human nature is, – who better? Well! He had a little money once, and he ran through it – as many men have done before him. He finds his old friends turn away from him now – many men have done that before him too! Shall he tell me why he writes to me? Because he has no kind of claim upon me. He puts it on that ground plainly; and begs to ask for the loan (as I know human nature) of two sovereigns, to be repaid next Tuesday six weeks, before twelve at noon.

Sometimes, when he is sure that I have found him out, and that there is no chance of money, he writes to inform me that I have got rid of him at last. He has enlisted into the Company's service, and is off directly – but he wants a cheese. He is informed by the sergeant that it is essential to his prospects in the regiment that he should take out a single-Gloucester cheese, weighing from twelve to fifteen pounds. Eight or nine shillings would buy it. He does not ask for money, after what has passed; but if he calls at nine, to-morrow morning may he hope to find a cheese? And is there anything he can do to show his gratitude in Bengal?

Once he wrote me rather a special letter, proposing relief in kind. He had got into a little trouble by leaving parcels of mud done up in brown paper, at people's houses, on pretence of being a Railway-Porter, in which character he received carriage money. This sportive fancy he expiated in the House of Correction. Not long after his release, and on a Sunday morning, he called with a letter (having first dusted himself all over), in which he gave me to understand that, being resolved to earn an honest livelihood, he had been travelling about the country with a cart of crockery. That he had been doing pretty well until the day before, when his horse had dropped down dead near Chatham, in Kent. That this had reduced him to the unpleasant necessity of getting into the shafts himself, and drawing the cart of crockery to London – a somewhat exhausting pull of thirty miles. That he did not venture to ask again for money; but that if I would have the goodness *to leave him out a donkey*, he would call for the animal before breakfast!

At another time my friend (I am describing actual experiences) introduced himself as a literary gentleman in the last extremity of distress. He had had a play accepted at a certain Theatre – which was really open; its representation was delayed by the indisposition of a leading actor – who was really ill; and he and his were in a state of absolute starvation. If he made his necessities known to the Manager of the Theatre, he put it to me to say what kind of treatment he might expect? Well! we got over that difficulty to our mutual satisfaction. A little while afterwards he was in some other strait – I think Mrs. Southcote, his wife, was in extremity – and we adjusted that point too. A little while afterwards, he had taken a new house, and was going headlong to ruin for want of a water-butt. I had my misgivings about the water- butt, and did not reply to that epistle. But a little while afterwards, I had reason to feel penitent for my neglect. He wrote me a few broken-hearted lines, informing me that the dear partner of his sorrows died in his arms last night at nine o'clock!

I despatched a trusty messenger to comfort the bereaved mourner and his poor children; but the messenger went so soon, that the play was not ready to be played out; my friend was not at home, and his wife was in a most delightful state of health. He was taken up by the Mendicity Society[23] (informally it afterwards appeared), and I presented myself at a London Police-Office with my testimony against him. The Magistrate was wonderfully struck by his educational acquirements, deeply impressed by the excellence of his letters, exceedingly sorry to see a man of his attainments there, complimented him highly on his powers of composition, and was quite charmed to have the agreeable duty of discharging him. A collection was made for the 'poor fellow,' as he was called in the reports, and I left the court with a com - fortable sense of being universally regarded as a sort of monster. Next day, comes to me a friend of mine, the governor of a large prison. 'Why did you ever go to the Police-Office against that man,' says he, 'without coming to me first? I know all about him and his frauds. He lodged in the house of one of my warders, at the very time when he first wrote to you; and then he was eating spring-lamb at eighteen-pence a pound, and early asparagus at I don't know how much a bundle!' On that very same day, and in that very same hour, my injured gentleman wrote a solemn address to me, demanding to know what compensation I proposed to make him for his having passed the night in a 'loathsome dungeon.' And next morning an Irish gentleman, a member of the same fraternity, who had read the case, and was very well persuaded I should be chary of going to that Police-Office again, positively refused to leave my door for less than a sovereign, and, resolved to besiege me into compliance, literally 'sat down' before it for ten mortal hours. The garrison being well provisioned, I remained within the walls; and he raised the siege at midnight with a prodigious alarum on the bell.

The Begging-Letter Writer often has an extensive circle of acquaintance. Whole pages of the 'Court Guide' are ready to be references for him. Noblemen and gentlemen write to say there never was such a man for probity and virtue. They have known him time out of mind, and there is nothing they wouldn't do for him. Somehow, they don't give him that one pound ten he stands in need of; but perhaps it is not enough – they want to do more, and his modesty will not allow it. It is to be remarked of his trade that it is a very fascinating one. He never leaves it; and those who are near to him become smitten with a love of it, too, and sooner or later set up for themselves. He employs a messenger – man, woman, or child. That messenger is certain ultimately to become an independent Begging-Letter Writer. His sons and daughters succeed to his calling, and write begging-letters when he is no more. He throws off the infection of begging-letter writing, like the contagion of disease. What Sydney Smith so happily called 'the dangerous luxury of dishonesty' is more tempting, and more catching, it would seem, in this instance than in any other.[24]

He always belongs to a Corresponding-Society of Begging-Letter Writers. Any one who will, may ascertain this fact. Give money to-day in recognition of a begging-letter, – no matter how unlike a common begging-letter, – and for the next fortnight you will have a rush of such communications. Steadily refuse to give; and the begging-letters become Angels' visits, until the Society is from some cause or other in a dull way of business, and may as well try you as anybody else. It is of little use inquiring into the Begging-Letter Writer's circumstances.

He may be sometimes accidentally found out, as in the case already mentioned (though that was not the first inquiry made); but apparent misery is always a part of his trade, and real misery very often is, in the intervals of spring-lamb and early asparagus. It is naturally an incident of his dissipated and dishonest life.

That the calling is a successful one, and that large sums of money are gained by it, must be evident to anybody who reads the Police Reports of such cases. But, prosecutions are of rare occurrence, relatively to the extent to which the trade is carried on. The cause of this is to be found (as no one knows better than the Begging-Letter Writer, for it is a part of his speculation) in the aversion people feel to exhibit themselves as having been imposed upon, or as having weakly gratified their consciences with a lazy, flimsy substitute for the noblest of all virtues. There is a man at large, at the moment when this paper is preparing for the press (on the 29th of April, 1850), and never once taken up yet, who, within these twelvemonths, has been probably the most audacious and the most successful swindler that even this trade has ever known. There has been something singularly base in this fellow's proceedings; it has been his business to write to all sorts and conditions of people, in the names of persons of high reputation and unblemished honour, professing to be in distress – the general admiration and respect for whom, has ensured a ready and generous reply.

Now, in the hope that the results of the real experience of a real person may do something more to induce reflection on this subject than any abstract treatise – and with a personal knowledge of the extent to which the Begging-Letter Trade has been carried on for some time, and has been for some time constantly increasing – the writer of this paper entreats the attention of his readers to a few concluding words. His experience is a type of the experience of many; some on a smaller; some on an infinitely larger scale. All may judge of the soundness or unsoundness of his conclusions from it.

Long doubtful of the efficacy of such assistance in any case whatever, and able to recall but one, within his whole individual knowledge, in which he had the least after-reason to suppose that any good was done by it, he was led, last autumn, into some serious considerations. The begging-letters flying about by every post, made it perfectly manifest, that a set of lazy vagabonds were interposed between the general desire to do something to relieve the sickness and misery under which the poor were suffering, and the suffering poor themselves. That many who sought to do some little to repair the social wrongs, inflicted in the way of preventible sickness and death upon the poor, were strengthening those wrongs, however innocently, by wasting money on pestilent knaves cumbering society. That imagination, – soberly following one of these knaves into his life of punishment in jail, and comparing it with the life of one of these poor in a cholera-stricken alley, or one of the children of one of these poor, soothed in its dying hour by the late lamented Mr. Drouet, – contemplated a grim farce, impossible to be presented very much longer before God or man. That the crowning miracle of all the miracles summed up in the New Testament, after the miracle of the blind seeing, and the lame walking, and the restoration of the dead to life, was the miracle that the poor had the Gospel preached to them. That while the poor were unnaturally and unnecessarily cut off by the thousand, in the prematurity of their age, or in the rottenness of their youth – for of flower or blossom such youth has none – the Gospel was NOT preached to them, saving in hollow and unmeaning voices. That of all wrongs, this was the first mighty wrong the Pestilence warned us to set right. And that no Post-Office Order to any amount, given to a Begging-Letter Writer for the quieting of an uneasy breast, would be presentable on the Last Great Day as anything towards it.

The poor never write these letters. Nothing could be more unlike their habits. The writers are public robbers; and we who support them are parties to their depredations. They trade upon every circumstance within their knowledge that affects us, public or private, joyful or sorrowful; they pervert the lessons of our lives; they change what ought to be our strength and virtue into weakness, and encouragement of vice. There is a plain remedy, and it is in our own hands. We must resolve, at any sacrifice of feeling, to be deaf to such appeals, and crush the trade.

There are degrees in murder. Life must be held sacred among us in more ways than one – sacred, not merely from the murderous weapon, or the subtle poison, or the cruel blow, but sacred from preventible diseases, distortions, and pains. That is the first great end we have to set against this miserable imposition. Physical life respected, moral life comes next. What will not content a Begging-Letter Writer for a week, would educate a score of children for a year. Let us give all we can; let us give more than ever. Let us do all we can; let us do more than ever. But let us give, and do, with a high purpose; not to endow the scum of the earth, to its own greater corruption, with the offals of our duty.

Wapping Workhouse

My day's no-business beckoning me to the East end of London, I had turned my face to that point of the metropolitan compass on leaving Covent Garden, and had got past the India House, thinking in my idle manner of Tippoo-Sahib and Charles Lamb,[25] and had got past my little wooden midshipman, after affectionately patting him on one leg of his knee-shorts for old acquaintance' sake, and had got past Aldgate Pump, and had got past the Saracen's Head[26] (with an ignominious rash of posting bills disfiguring his swarthy countenance), and had strolled up the empty yard of his ancient neighbour the Black or Blue Boar, or Bull, who departed this life I don't know when, and whose coaches are all gone I don't know where; and I had come out again into the age of railways, and I had got past Whitechapel Church, and was – rather inappropriately for an Uncommercial Traveller – in the Commercial Road. Pleasantly wallowing in the abundant mud of that thoroughfare, and greatly enjoying the huge piles of building belonging to the sugar refiners, the little masts and vanes in small back gardens in back streets, the neighbouring canals and docks, the India vans lumbering along their stone tramway, and the pawnbrokers' shops where hard-up Mates had pawned so many sextants and quadrants, that I should have bought a few cheap if I had the least notion how to use them, I at last began to file off to the right, towards Wapping.

Not that I intended to take boat at Wapping Old Stairs, or that I was going to look at the locality, because I believe (for I don't) in the constancy of the young woman who told her sea-going lover, to such a beautiful old tune, that she had ever continued the same, since she gave him the 'baccer-box marked with his name; I am afraid he usually got the worst of those transactions, and was frightfully taken in.[27] No, I was going to Wapping, because an Eastern police magistrate had said, through the morning papers, that there was no classification at the Wapping workhouse for women, and that it was a disgrace and a shame and divers other hard names, and because I wished to see how the fact really stood. For, that Eastern police magistrates are not always the wisest men of the East, may be inferred from their course of procedure respecting the fancy-dressing and pantomime-posturing at St. George's in that quarter: which is usually, to discuss the matter at issue, in a state of mind betokening the weakest perplexity, with all parties concerned and unconcerned, and, for a final expedient, to consult the complainant as to what he thinks ought to be done with the defendant, and take the defendant's opinion as to what he would recommend to be done with himself.

Long before I reached Wapping, I gave myself up as having lost my way, and, abandoning myself to the narrow streets in a Turkish frame of mind, relied on predestination to bring me somehow or other to the place I wanted if I were ever to get there. When I had ceased for an hour or so to take any trouble about the matter, I found myself on a swing-bridge, looking down at some dark locks in some dirty water. Over against me, stood a creature remotely in the likeness of a young man, with a puffed sallow face, and a figure all dirty and shiny and slimy, who may have been the youngest son of his filthy old father, Thames, or the drowned man about whom there was a placard on the granite post like a large thimble, that stood between us.

I asked this apparition what it called the place? Unto which, it replied, with a ghastly grin and a sound like gurgling water in its throat:

'Mister Baker's trap.'

As it is a point of great sensitiveness with me on such occasions to be equal to the intellectual pressure of the conversation, I deeply considered the meaning of this speech, while I eyed the apparition – then engaged in hugging and sucking a horizontal iron bar at the top of the locks. Inspiration suggested to me that Mr. Baker was the acting Coroner of that neighbourhood.

'A common place for suicide,' said I, looking down at the locks.

'Sue?' returned the ghost, with a stare. 'Yes! And Poll. Like - wise Emily. And Nancy. And Jane;' he sucked the iron between each name; 'and all the bileing. Ketches off their bonnets or shorls, takes a run, and headers down here, they doos. Always a headerin' down here, they is. Like one o'clock.'

'And at about that hour of the morning, I suppose?'

'Ah!' said the apparition. '*They* an't partickler. Two 'ull do for *them*. Three. All times o' night. On'y mind you!' Here the apparition rested his profile on the bar, and gurgled in a sarcastic manner. 'There must be somebody comin'. They don't go a headerin' down here, wen there an't no Bobby nor gen'ral Cove, fur to hear the splash.'

According to my interpretation of these words, I was myself a General Cove, or member of the miscellaneous public. In which modest character I remarked:

'They are often taken out, are they, and restored?'

'I dunno about restored,' said the apparition, who, for some occult reason, very much objected to that word; 'they're carried into the werkiss and put into a 'ot bath, and brought round. But I dunno about restored,' said the apparition; 'blow *that*!' – and vanished.

As it had shown a desire to become offensive, I was not sorry to find myself alone, especially as the 'werkiss' it had indicated with a twist of its matted head, was close at hand. So I left Mr. Baker's terrible trap (baited with a scum that was like the soapy rinsing of sooty chimneys), and made bold to ring at the workhouse gate, where I was wholly unexpected and quite unknown.

A very bright and nimble little matron, with a bunch of keys in her hand, responded to my request to see the House. I began to doubt whether the police magistrate was quite right in his facts, when I noticed her quick, active little figure and her intelligent eyes.

The Traveller (the matron intimated) should see the worst first. He was welcome to see everything. Such as it was, there it all was.

This was the only preparation for our entering 'the Foul wards.' They were in an old building squeezed away in a corner of a paved yard, quite detached from the more modern and spacious main body of the workhouse. They were in a building most monstrously behind the time – a mere series of garrets or lofts, with every inconvenient and objectionable circumstance in their construction, and only accessible by steep and narrow staircases, infamously ill-adapted for the passage up-stairs of the sick or down stairs of the dead.

A-bed in these miserable rooms, here on bedsteads, there (for a change, as I understood it) on the floor, were women in every stage of distress and disease. None but those who have attentively observed such scenes, can conceive the extraordinary variety of expression still latent under the general monotony and uniformity of colour, attitude, and condition. The form a little coiled up and turned away, as though it had turned its back on this world for ever; the uninterested face at once lead-coloured and yellow, looking passively upward from the pillow; the haggard mouth a little dropped, the hand outside the coverlet, so dull and indifferent, so light, and yet so heavy; these were on every pallet; but when I stopped beside a bed, and said ever so slight a word to the figure lying there, the ghost of the old character came into the face, and made the Foul ward as various as the fair world. No one appeared to care to live, but no one complained; all who could speak, said that as much was done for them as could be done there, that the attendance was kind and patient, that their suffering was very heavy, but they had nothing to ask for. The wretched rooms were as clean and sweet as it is possible for such rooms to be; they would become a pest-house in a single week, if they were ill-kept.

I accompanied the brisk matron up another barbarous staircase, into a better kind of loft devoted to the idiotic and imbecile. There was at least Light in it, whereas the windows in the former wards had been like sides of school-boys' bird-cages. There was a strong grating over the fire here, and, holding a kind of state on either side of the hearth, separated by the breadth of this grating, were two old ladies in a condition of feeble dignity, which was surely the very last and lowest reduction of self-complacency to be found in this wonderful humanity of ours. They were evidently jealous of each other, and passed their whole time (as some people do, whose fires are not grated) in mentally disparaging each other, and contemptuously watching their neighbours. One of these parodies on provincial gentlewomen was extremely talkative, and expressed a strong desire to attend the service on Sundays, from which she represented herself to have derived the greatest interest and consolation when allowed that privilege. She gossiped so well, and looked altogether so cheery and harmless, that I began to think this a case for the Eastern magistrate, until I found that on the last occasion of her attending chapel she had secreted a small stick, and had caused some confusion in the responses by suddenly producing it and belabouring the congregation.

So, these two old ladies, separated by the breadth of the grating – otherwise they would fly at one another's caps – sat all day long, suspecting one another, and contemplating a world of fits. For everybody else in the room had fits, except the wards-woman; an elderly, able-bodied pauperess, with a large upper lip, and an air of repressing and saving her strength, as she stood with her hands folded before her, and her eyes slowly rolling, biding her time for catching or holding somebody. This civil personage (in whom I regretted to identify a reduced member of my honourable friend Mrs. Gamp's family)[28] said, 'They has 'em continiwal, sir. They drops without no more notice than if they was coach-horses dropped from the moon, sir. And when one drops, another drops, and sometimes there'll be as many as four or five on 'em at once, dear me, a rolling and a tearin', bless you! – this young woman, now, has 'em dreadful bad.'

She turned up this young woman's face with her hand as she said it. This young woman was seated on the floor, pondering, in the foreground of the afflicted. There was nothing repellent either in her face or head. Many, apparently worse, varieties of epilepsy and hysteria were about her, but she was said to be the worst here. When I had spoken to her a little, she still sat with her face turned up, pondering, and a gleam of the mid-day sun shone in upon her.

– Whether this young woman, and the rest of these so sorely troubled, as they sit or lie pondering in their confused dull way, ever get mental glimpses among the motes in the sunlight, of healthy people and healthy things? Whether this young woman, brooding like this in the summer season, ever thinks that somewhere there are trees and flowers, even mountains and the great sea? Whether, not to go so far, this young woman ever has any dim revelation of that young woman – that young woman who is not here and never will come here; who is courted, and caressed, and loved, and has a husband, and bears children, and lives in a home, and who never knows what it is to have this lashing and tearing coming upon her? And whether this young woman, God help her, gives herself up then and drops like a coach-horse from the moon?

I hardly knew whether the voices of infant children, penetrating into so hopeless a place, made a sound that was pleasant or painful to me. It was something to be reminded that the weary world was not all weary, and was ever renewing itself; but, this young woman was a child not long ago, and a child not long hence might be such as she. Howbeit, the active step and eye of the vigilant matron conducted me past the two provincial gentlewomen (whose dignity was ruffled by the children), and into the adjacent nursery.

There were many babies here, and more than one handsome young mother. There were ugly young mothers also, and sullen young mothers, and callous young mothers. But, the babies had not appropriated to themselves any bad expression yet, and might have been, for anything that appeared to the contrary in their soft faces, Princes Imperial, and Princesses Royal. I had the pleasure of giving a poetical commission to the baker's man to make a cake with all despatch and toss it into the oven for one red-headed young pauper and myself, and felt much the better for it. Without that refreshment, I doubt if I should have been in a condition for 'the Refractories,'[29] towards whom my quick little matron – for whose adaptation to her office I had by this time conceived a genuine respect – drew me next, and marshalled me the way that I was going.

The Refractories were picking oakum, in a small room giving on a yard. They sat in line on a form, with their backs to a window; before them, a table, and their work. The oldest Refractory was, say twenty; youngest Refractory, say sixteen. I have never yet ascertained in the course of my uncommercial travels, why a Refractory habit should affect the tonsils and uvula; but, I have always observed that Refractories of both sexes and every grade, between a Ragged School and the Old Bailey, have one voice, in which the tonsils and uvula gain a diseased ascendency.

'Five pound indeed! I hain't a going fur to pick five pound,' said the Chief of the Refractories, keeping time to herself with her head and chin. 'More than enough to pick what we picks now, in sitch a place as this, and on wot we gets here!'

(This was in acknowledgment of a delicate intimation that the amount of work was likely to be increased. It certainly was not heavy then, for one Refractory had already done her day's task – it was barely two o'clock – and was sitting behind it, with a head exactly matching it.)

'A pretty Ouse this is, matron, ain't it?' said Refractory Two, 'where a pleeseman's called in, if a gal says a word!'

'And wen you're sent to prison for nothink or less!' said the Chief, tugging at her oakum as if it were the matron's hair. 'But any place is better than this; that's one thing, and be thankful!'

A laugh of Refractories led by Oakum Head with folded arms – who originated nothing, but who was in command of the skirmishers outside the conversation.

'If any place is better than this,' said my brisk guide, in the calmest manner, 'it is a pity you left a good place when you had one.'

'Ho, no, I didn't, matron,' returned the Chief, with another pull at her oakum, and a very expressive look at the enemy's forehead. 'Don't say that, matron, 'cos it's lies!'

Oakum Head brought up the skirmishers again, skirmished, and retired.

'And *I* warn't a going,' exclaimed Refractory Two, 'though I was in one place for as long as four year – *I* warn't a going fur to stop in a place that warn't fit for me – there! And where the family warn't 'spectable characters – there! And where I fortunately or hunfort'nately, found that the people warn't what they pretended to make theirselves out to be – there! And where it wasn't their faults, by chalks, if I warn't made bad and ruinated – Hah!'

During this speech, Oakum Head had again made a diversion with the skirmishers, and had again withdrawn.

The Uncommercial Traveller ventured to remark that he supposed Chief Refractory and Number One, to be the two young women who had been taken before the magistrate?

'Yes!' said the Chief, 'we har! and the wonder is, that a plees - eman an't 'ad in now, and we took off agen. You can't open your lips here, without a pleeseman.'

Number Two laughed (very uvularly), and the skirmishers followed suit.

'I'm sure I'd be thankful,' protested the Chief, looking sideways at the Uncommercial, 'if I could be got into a place, or got abroad. I'm sick and tired of this precious Ouse, I am, with reason.'

So would be, and so was, Number Two. So would be, and so was, Oakum Head. So would be, and so were, Skirmishers.

The Uncommercial took the liberty of hinting that he hardly thought it probable that any lady or gentleman in want of a likely young domestic of retiring manners, would be tempted into the engagement of either of the two leading Refractories, on her own presentation of herself as per sample.

'It ain't no good being nothink else here,' said the Chief.

The Uncommercial thought it might be worth trying.

'Oh no it ain't,' said the Chief.

'Not a bit of good,' said Number Two.

'And I'm sure I'd be very thankful to be got into a place, or got abroad,' said the Chief.

'And so should I,' said Number Two. 'Truly thankful, I should.'

Oakum Head then rose, and announced as an entirely new idea, the mention of which profound novelty might be naturally expected to startle her unprepared hearers, that she would be very thankful to be got into a place, or got abroad. And, as if she had then said, 'Chorus, ladies!' all the Skirmishers struck up to the same purpose. We left them, thereupon, and began a long walk among the women who were simply old and infirm; but whenever, in the course of this same walk, I looked out of any high window that commanded the yard, I saw Oakum Head and all the other Refractories looking out at their low window for me, and never failing to catch me, the moment I showed my head.

In ten minutes I had ceased to believe in such fables of a golden time as youth, the prime of life, or a hale old age. In ten minutes, all the lights of womankind seemed to have been blown out, and nothing in that way to be left this vault to brag of, but the flickering and expiring snuffs.

And what was very curious, was, that these dim old women had one company notion which was the fashion of the place. Every old woman who became aware of a visitor and was not in bed hobbled over a form into her accustomed seat, and became one of a line of dim old women confronting another line of dim old women across a narrow table. There was no obligation whatever upon them to range themselves in this way; it was their manner of 'receiving.' As a rule, they made no attempt to talk to one another, or to look at the visitor, or to look at anything, but sat silently working their mouths, like a sort of poor old Cows. In some of these wards, it was good to see a few green plants; in others, an isolated Refractory acting as nurse, who did well enough in that capacity, when separated from her compeers; every one of these wards, day room, night room, or both combined, was scrupulously clean and fresh. I have seen as many such places as most travellers in my line, and I never saw one such, better kept.

Among the bedridden there was great patience, great reliance on the books under the pillow, great faith in GOD. All cared for sympathy, but none much cared to be encouraged with hope of recovery; on the whole, I should say, it was considered rather a distinction to have a complication of disorders, and to be in a worse way than the rest. From some of the windows, the river could be seen with all its life and movement; the day was bright, but I came upon no one who was looking out.

In one large ward, sitting by the fire in arm-chairs of distinction, like the President and Vice of the good company, were two old women, upwards of ninety years of age. The younger of the two, just turned ninety, was deaf, but not very, and could easily be made to hear. In her early time she had nursed a child, who was now another old woman, more infirm than herself, inhabiting the very same chamber. She perfectly understood this when the matron told it, and, with sundry nods and motions of her forefinger, pointed out the woman in question. The elder of this pair, ninety-three, seated before an illustrated newspaper (but not reading it), was a bright-eyed old soul, really not deaf, wonderfully preserved, and amazingly conversational. She had not long lost her husband, and had been in that place little more than a year. At Boston, in the State of Massachusetts, this poor creature would have been individually addressed, would have been tended in her own room, and would have had her life gently assimilated to a comfortable life out of doors. Would that be much to do in England for a woman who has kept herself out of a workhouse more than ninety rough long years? When

Britain first, at Heaven's command, arose, with a great deal of allegorical confusion, from out the azure main, did her guardian angels positively forbid it in the Charter which has been so much be-sung?

The object of my journey was accomplished when the nimble matron had no more to show me. As I shook hands with her at the gate, I told her that I thought Justice had not used her very well, and that the wise men of the East were not infallible.

Now, I reasoned with myself, as I made my journey home again, concerning those Foul wards. They ought not to exist; no person of common decency and humanity can see them and doubt it. But what is this Union to do? The necessary alteration would cost several thousands of pounds; it has already to support three workhouses; its inhabitants work hard for their bare lives, and are already rated for the relief of the Poor to the utmost extent of reasonable endurance. One poor parish in this very Union is rated to the amount of FIVE AND SIXPENCE in the pound, at the very same time when the rich parish of Saint George's, Hanover-square, is rated at about SEVENPENCE in the pound, Paddington at about FOURPENCE, Saint James's, Westminster, at about TENPENCE! It is only through the equalisation of Poor Rates that what is left undone in this wise, can be done. Much more is left undone, or is ill-done, than I have space to suggest in these notes of a single uncommercial journey; but, the wise men of the East, before they can reasonably hold forth about it, must look to the North and South and West; let them also, any morning before taking the seat of Solomon, look into the shops and dwellings all around the Temple, and first ask themselves 'how much more can these poor people – many of whom keep themselves with difficulty enough out of the workhouse – bear?'

I had yet other matter for reflection as I journeyed home, inasmuch as, before I altogether departed from the neighbourhood of Mr. Baker's trap, I had knocked at the gate of the workhouse of St. George's-in-the-East, and had found it to be an establishment highly creditable to those parts, and thoroughly well administered by a most intelligent master. I remarked in it, an instance of the collateral harm that obstinate vanity and folly can do. 'This was the Hall where those old paupers, male and female, whom I had just seen, met for the Church service, was it?' – 'Yes.' – 'Did they sing the Psalms to any instrument?' – 'They would like to, very much; they would have an extraordinary interest in doing so.' – 'And could none be got?' – 'Well, a piano could even have been got for nothing, but these unfortunate dissensions –' Ah! better, far better, my Christian friend in the beautiful garment, to have let the singing boys alone, and left the multitude to sing for themselves! You should know better than I, but I think I have read that they did so, once upon a time, and that 'when they had sung an hymn,' Some one (not in a beautiful garment) went up into the Mount of Olives.

It made my heart ache to think of this miserable trifling, in the streets of a city where every stone seemed to call to me, as I walked along, 'Turn this way, man, and see what waits to be done!' So I decoyed myself into another train of thought to ease my heart. But, I don't know that I did it, for I was so full of paupers, that it was, after all, only a change to a single pauper, who took possession of my remembrance instead of a thousand.

'I beg your pardon, sir,' he had said, in a confidential manner, on another occasion, taking me aside; 'but I have seen better days.'

'I am very sorry to hear it.'

'Sir, I have a complaint to make against the master.'

'I have no power here, I assure you. And if I had –'

'But, allow me, sir, to mention it, as between yourself and a man who has seen better days, sir. The master and myself are both masons, sir, and I make him the sign continually; but, because I am in this unfortunate position, sir, he won't give me the countersign!'

Home for Homeless Women

Five years and a half ago, certain ladies, grieved to think that numbers of their own sex were wandering about the streets in degradation, passing through and through the prisons all their lives, or hopelessly perishing in other ways, resolved to try the experiment on a limited scale of a Home for the reclamation and emigration of women. As it was clear to them that there could be little or no hope in this country for the greater part of those who might become the objects of their charity, they determined to receive into their Home, only those who distinctly accepted this condition: That they came there to be ultimately sent abroad (whither, was at the discretion of the ladies); and that they also came there, to remain for such length of time as might, according to the circumstances of each individual case, be considered necessary as a term of probation, and for instruction in the means of obtaining an honest livelihood. The object of the Home was twofold. First, to replace young women who had already lost their characters and lapsed into guilt, in a situation of hope. Secondly, to save other young women who were in danger of falling into the like condition, and give them an opportunity of flying from crime when they and it stood face to face.

The projectors of this establishment, in undertaking it, were sustained by nothing but the high object of making some unhappy women a blessing to themselves and others instead of a curse, and raising up among the solitudes of a new world some virtuous homes, much needed there, from the sorrow and ruin of the old. They had no romantic visions or extravagant expectations. They were prepared for many failures and disappointments, and to consider their enterprise rewarded, if they in time succeeded with one third or one half of the cases they received.

As the experience of this small Institution, even under the many disadvantages of a beginning, may be useful and interesting, this paper will contain an exact account of its progress and results.

It was (and is) established in a detached house with a garden. The house was never designed for any such purpose, and is only adapted to it, in being retired and not immediately overlooked. It is capable of containing thirteen inmates besides two Superintendents. Excluding from consideration ten young women now in the house, there have been received in all, since November eighteen hundred and forty-seven, fifty-six inmates. They have belonged to no particular class, but have been starving needle women of good character, poor needlewomen who have robbed their furnished lodgings, violent girls committed to prison for disturbances in ill-conducted workhouses, poor girls from Ragged Schools, destitute girls who have applied at Police offices for relief, young women from the streets: young women of the same class taken from the prisons after undergoing punishment there as disorderly characters, or for shoplifting, or for thefts from the person: domestic servants who have been seduced, and two young women held to bail for attempting suicide. No class has been favoured more than another; and misfortune and distress are a sufficient introduction. It is not usual to receive women of more than five or six-and-twenty; the average age in the fifty-six cases would probably be about twenty. In some instances there have been great personal attractions; in others, the girls have been very homely and plain. The reception has been wholly irrespective of such sources of interest. Nearly all have been extremely ignorant.

Of these fifty-six cases, seven went away by their own desire during their probation; ten were sent away for misconduct in the Home; seven ran away; three emigrated and relapsed on the passage out; thirty (of whom seven are now married) on their arrival in Australia or elsewhere, entered into good service, acquired a good character, and have done so well ever since as to establish a strong prepossession in favour of others sent out from the same quarter. It will be seen from these figures that the failures are generally discovered in the Home itself, and that the amount of misconduct after the training and emigration, is remarkably small. And it is to be taken into consideration that many cases are admitted into the Home, of which there is, in the outset, very little hope, but which it is not deemed right to exclude from the experiment.

The Home is managed by two Superintendents. The second in order acts under the first, who has from day to day the supreme direction of the family. On the cheerfulness, quickness, good-temper, firmness, and vigilance of these ladies, and on their never bickering, the successful working of the establishment in a great degree depends. Their position is one of high trust and responsibility, and requires not only an always accumulating experience, but an accurate observation of every character about them. The ladies who established the Home, hold little confidential communication with the inmates, thinking the system better administered when it is undisturbed by individuals. A committee, composed of a few gentlemen of experience, meets once a month to audit the accounts, receive the principal Superintendent's reports, investigate any unusual occurrence, and see all the inmates separately. None but the committee are present as they enter one by one, in order that they may be under no restraint in anything they wish to say. A complaint from any of them is exceedingly uncommon. The history of every inmate, taken down from her own mouth – usually after she has been some little time in the Home – is preserved in a book.[30] She is shown that what she relates of herself she relates in confidence, and does not even communicate to the Superintendents. She is particularly admonished by no means to communicate her history to any of the other inmates: all of whom have in their turns received a similar admonition. And she is encouraged to tell the truth, by having it explained to her that nothing in her story but falsehood, can possibly affect her position in the Home after she has been once admitted.

The work of the Home is thus divided. They rise, both in summer and winter, at six o'clock. Morning prayers and scripture reading take place at a quarter before eight. Breakfast is had immediately afterwards. Dinner at one. Tea at six. Evening prayers are said at half-past eight. The hour of going to bed is nine. Supposing the Home to be full, ten are employed upon the household work; two in the bedrooms; two in the general living room; two in the Superintendents' rooms; two in the kitchen (who cook); two in the scullery; three at needle-work. Straw-plaiting has been occasionally taught besides. On washing-days, five are employed in the laundry, three of whom are taken from the needle-work, and two are told off from the household work. The nature and order of each girl's work is changed every week, so that she may become practically acquainted with the whole routine of household duties. They take it in turns to bake the bread which is eaten in the house. In every room, every Monday morning, there is hung up, framed and glazed, the names of the girls who are in charge there for the week and who are, consequently, responsible for its neat condition and the proper execution of the work belonging to it. This is found to inspire them with a greater pride in good housewifery, and a greater sense of shame in the reverse.

The book-education is of a very plain kind, as they have generally much to learn in the commonest domestic duties, and are often singularly inexpert in acquiring them. They read and write, and cypher. School is held every morning at half-past ten (Saturday excepted) for two hours. The Superintendents are the teachers. The times for recreation are half an hour between school-time and dinner, and an hour after dinner; half an hour before tea, and an hour after tea. In the winter, these intervals are usually employed in light fancy work, the making of little presents for their friends, &c. In the fine summer weather they are passed in the garden, where they take exercise, and have their little flower-beds. In the afternoon and evening, they sit all together at needlework, and some one reads aloud. The books are carefully chosen, but are always interesting.

Saturday is devoted to an extraordinary cleaning up and polishing of the whole establishment, and to the distribution of clean clothes; every inmate arranging and preparing her own. Each girl also takes a bath on Saturday.

On Sundays they go to church in the neighbourhood, some to morning service, some to afternoon service, some to both. They are invariably accompanied by one of the Superintendents. Wearing no uniform and not being dressed alike, they attract little notice out of doors. Their attire is that of respectable plain servants. On Sunday evenings they receive religious instruction from the principal Superintendent. They also receive regular religious instruction from a clergyman on one day in every week, and on two days in every alternate week. They are constantly employed, and always overlooked.

They are allowed to be visited under the following restrictions; if by their parents, once in a month; if by other relatives or friends, once in three months. The principal Superintendent is present at all such interviews, and hears the conversation. It is not often found that the girls and their friends have much to say to one another; any display of feeling on these occasions is rare. It is generally observed that the inmates seem rather relieved than otherwise when the interviews are over.

They can write to relatives, or old teachers, or persons known to have been kind to them, once a month on application to the committee. It seldom happens that a girl who has any person in the world to correspond with, fails to take advantage of this opportunity. All letters dispatched from the Home are read and posted by the principal Superintendent. All letters received, are likewise read by the Superintendent; but she does not open them. Every such letter is opened by the girl to whom it is addressed, who reads it first, in the Superintendent's presence. It never happens that they wish to reserve the contents; they are always anxious to impart them to her immediately. This seems to be one of their chief pleasures in receiving letters.

They make and mend their own clothes, but do not keep them. In many cases they are not for some time to be trusted with such a charge; in other cases, when temper is awakened, the possession of a shawl and bonnet would often lead to an abrupt departure which the unfortunate creature would ever afterwards regret. To distinguish between these cases and others of a more promising nature, would be to make invidious distinctions, than which nothing could be more prejudicial to the Home, as the objects of its care are invariably sensitive and jealous. For these various reasons their clothes are kept under lock and key in a wardrobe room. They have a great pride in the state of their clothes, and the neatness of their persons. Those who have no such pride on their admission, are sure to acquire it.

Formerly, when a girl accepted for admission had clothes of her own to wear, she was allowed to be admitted in them, and they were put by for her; though within the Institution she always wore the clothing it provides. It was found, however, that a girl with a hankering after old companions rather relied on these reserved clothes, and that she put them on with an air, if she went away or were dismissed. They now invariably come, therefore, in clothes belonging to the Home, and bring no other clothing with them. A suit of the commonest apparel has been provided for the next inmate who may leave during her probation, or be sent away; and it is thought that the sight of a girl departing so disgraced, will have a good effect on those who remain. Cases of dismissal or departure are becoming more rare, however, as the Home increases in experience, and no occasion for making the experiment has yet arisen.

When the Home had been opened for some time, it was resolved to adopt a modification of Captain Maconochie's mark system:[31] so arranging the mark table as to render it difficult for a girl to lose marks under any one of its heads, without also losing under nearly all the others. The mark table is divided into the nine following heads. Truthfulness, Industry, Temper,

Propriety of Conduct and Conversation, Temperance, Order, Punctuality, Economy, Cleanliness. The word Temperance is not used in the modern slang acceptation,[32] but in its enlarged meaning as defined by Johnson, from the English of Spenser: 'Moderation, patience, calmness, sedateness, moderation of passion.' A separate account for every day is kept with every girl as to each of these items. If her conduct be without objection, she is marked in each column, three – excepting the truthfulness and temperance columns, in which, saving under extraordinary circumstances, she is only marked two: the temptation to err in those particulars, being considered low under the circumstances of the life she leads in the Home. If she be particularly deserving under any of the other heads, she is marked the highest number four. If her deserts be low, she is marked only one, or not marked at all. If her conduct under any head have been, during the day, particularly objectionable, she receives a bad mark (marked in red ink, to distinguish it at a glance from the others) which destroys forty good marks. The value of the good marks is six shillings and sixpence per thousand; the earnings of each girl are withheld until she emigrates, in order to form a little fund for her first subsistence on her disembarkation. The inmates are found, without an exception, to value their marks highly. A bad mark is very infrequent, and occasions great distress in the recipient and great excitement in the community. In case of dismissal or premature departure from the Home, all the previous gain in marks is forfeited. If a girl be ill through no fault of her own, she is marked, during her illness, according to her average marking. But, if she be ill through her own act (as in a recent case, where a girl set herself on fire, through carelessness and a violation of the rules of the house) she is credited with no marks until she is again in a condition to earn them. The usual earnings in a year are about equal to the average wages of the commoner class of domestic servant.

They are usually brought to the Home by the principal Superintendent in a coach. From wheresoever they come, they generally weep on the road, and are silent and depressed. The average term of probation is about a year; longer when the girl is very slow to learn what she is taught. When the time of her emigration arrives, the same lady accompanies her on board ship. They usually go out, three or four together, with a letter of recommendation to some influential person at their destination; sometimes they are placed under the charge of a respectable family of emigrants; sometimes they act as nurses or as servants to individual ladies with children, on board. In these capacities they have given great satisfaction. Their grief at parting from the Superintendent is always strong, and frequently of a heart-rending kind. They are also exceedingly affected by their separation from the Home; usually going round and round the garden first, as if they clung to every tree and shrub in it. Nevertheless, individual attachments among them are rare, though strong affections have arisen when they have afterwards encountered in distant solitudes. Some touching circumstances have occurred, where unexpected recognitions of this kind have taken place on Sundays in lonely churches to which the various members of the little congregations have repaired from great distances. Some of the girls now married have chosen old companions thus encountered for their bridesmaids, and in their letters have described their delight very pathetically.

A considerable part of the needle-work done in the Home is necessary to its own internal neatness, and the preparation of outfits for the emigrants; especially as many of the inmates know little or nothing of such work, and have it all to learn. But, as they become more dexterous, plain work is taken in, and the proceeds are applied as a fund to defray the cost of outfits. The outfits are always of the simplest kind. Nothing is allowed to be wasted or thrown away in the Home. From the bones, and remnants of food, the girls are taught to make soup for the poor and sick. This at once extends their domestic knowledge, and preserves their sympathy for the distressed.

Some of the experiences, not already mentioned, that have been acquired in the management of the Home are curious, and perhaps deserving of consideration in prisons and other institutions. It has been observed, in taking the histories – especially of the more artful cases – that nothing is so likely to elicit the truth as a perfectly imperturbable face, and an avoidance of any leading question or expression of opinion. Give the narrator the least idea what tone will make her an object of interest, and she will take it directly. Give her none, and she will be driven on the truth, and in most cases will tell it. For similar reasons it is found desirable always to repress stock religious professions and religious phrases; to discourage shows of sentiment, and to make their lives practical and active. 'Don't talk about it – do it!' is the motto of the place. The inmates find everywhere about them the same kind, discriminating firmness, and the same determination to have no favourite subjects, or favourite objects, of interest. Girls from Ragged Schools are not generally so impressible as reduced girls who have failed to support themselves by hard work, or as women from the streets – probably, because they have suffered less. The poorest of the Ragged School condition, who are odious to approach when first picked up, invariably affect afterwards that their friends are 'well off.' This psychological curiosity is considered inexplicable. Most of the inmates are depressed at first. At holiday times the more doubtful part of them usually become restless and uncertain; there would also appear to be, usually, a time of considerable restlessness after six or eight months. In any little difficulty, the general feeling is invariably with the establishment and never with the offender. When a girl is discharged for misconduct, she is generally in deep distress, and goes away miserably. The rest will sometimes intercede for her with tears; but it is found that firmness on this and every point, when a decision is once taken, is the most humane course as having a wholesome influence on the greatest number. For this reason, a mere threat of discharge is never on any account resorted to. Two points of management are extremely important; the first, to refer very sparingly to the past; the second, never to treat the inmates as children. They must never be allowed to suppose it possible that they can get the better of the management. Judicious commendation, when it is deserved, has a very salutary influence. It is also found that a serious and urgent entreaty to a girl, to exercise her self-restraint on some point (generally temper) on which her mark-table shews her to be deficient, often has an excellent effect when it is accompanied with such encouragement as, 'You know how changed you are since you have been here; you know we have begun to entertain great hopes of you. For God's sake consider! Do not throw away this great chance of your life, by making yourself and everybody around you unhappy – which will oblige us to send you away – but conquer this. Now, try hard for a month, and pray let us have no fault to find with you at the end of that time.' Many will make great and successful efforts to control themselves, after such remonstrance. In all cases, the fewest and plainest words are the best. When new to the place, they are found to break and spoil through great carelessness. Patience, and the strictest attention to order and punctuality, will in most cases overcome these discouragements. Nothing else will. They are often rather disposed to quarrel among themselves, particularly in bad weather when their lives are necessarily monotonous and confined; but, on the whole, allowing for their different breeding, they perhaps quarrel less than the average of passengers in the state cabin on a voyage out to India.

As some of the inmates of the Home have to be saved and guarded from themselves more than from any other people, they can scarcely be defended by too many precautions. These precautions are not obtruded upon them, but are strictly observed. Keys are never left about. The garden gate is always kept locked; but the girls take it in turn to act as porteress, overlooked by the second superintendent. They are proud of this trust. Any inmate missing from her usual place for ten minutes would be looked after. Any suspicious circumstance would be quickly and quietly investigated. As no girl makes her own bed, no girl has the opportunity of safely hiding any secret correspondence, or anything else, in it. Each inmate has a separate bed, but there are several beds in a room. The occupants of each room are always arranged with a reference to their several characters and counteracting influences. A girl declaring that she wishes to leave, is not allowed to do so hastily, but is locked in a chamber by herself, to consider of it until next day: when, if she still persist, she is formally discharged. It has never once happened that a girl, however excited, has refused to submit to this restraint.

One of the most remarkable effects of the Home, even in many of the cases where it does not ultimately succeed, is the extraordinary change it produces in the appearance of its inmates. Putting out of the question their look of cleanliness and health (which may be regarded as a physical consequence of their treatment) a refining and humanising alteration is wrought in the expression of the features, and in the whole air of the person, which can scarcely be imagined. Teachers in Ragged Schools have made the observation in reference to young women whom they had previously known well, and for a long time. A very sagacious and observant police magistrate, visiting a girl before her emigration who had been taken from his bar, could detect no likeness in her to the girl he remembered. It is considered doubtful whether, in the majority of the worst cases, the subject would easily be known again at a year's end, among a dozen, by an old companion.

The moral influence of the Home, still applying the remark even to cases of failure, is illustrated in a no less remarkable manner. It has never had any violence done to a chair or a stool. It has never been asked to render any aid to the one lady and her assistant, who are shut up with the thirteen the year round. Bad language is so uncommon, that its utterance is an event. The committee have never heard the least approach to it, or seen anything but submission; though it has often been their task to reprove and dismiss women who have been violently agitated, and unquestionably (for the time) incensed against them. Four of the fugitives have robbed the Institution of some clothes. The rest had no reason on earth for running away in preference to asking to be dismissed, but shame in not remaining.

A specimen or two of cases of success may be interesting.

Case number twenty-seven, was a girl supposed to be of about eighteen, but who had none but supposititious knowledge of her age, and no knowledge at all of her birthday. Both her parents had died in her infancy. She had been brought up in the establishment of that amiable victim of popular prejudice, the late Mr. Drouet, of Tooting. It did not appear that she was naturally stupid, but her intellect had been so dulled by neglect that she was in the Home many months before she could be imbued with a thorough understanding that Christmas Day was so called as the birthday of Jesus Christ. But when she acquired this piece of learning, she was amazingly proud of it. She had been apprenticed to a small artificial flower maker with three others. They were all ill-treated, and all seemed to have run away at different times: this girl last: who absconded with an old man, a hawker, who brought 'combs and things' to the door for sale. She took what she called 'some old clothes' of her mistress with her, and was apprehended with the old man, and they were tried together. He was acquitted; she was found guilty. Her sentence was six months' imprisonment, and, on its expiration, she was received into the Home. She was appallingly ignorant, but most anxious to learn, and contended against her blunted faculties with a consciously slow perseverance. She showed a remarkable capacity for copying writing by the eye alone, without having the least idea of its sound, or what it meant. There seemed to be some analogy between her making letters and her making artificial flowers. She remained in the Home, bearing an excellent character, about a year. On her passage out, she made artificial flowers for the ladies on board, earned money, and was much liked. She obtained a comfortable service as soon as she landed, and is happy and respected. This girl had not a friend in the world, and had never known a natural affection, or formed a natural tie, upon the face of this earth.

Case number thirteen was a half-starved girl of eighteen whose father had died soon after her birth, and who had long eked out a miserable subsistence for herself and a sick mother by doing plain needlework. At last her mother died in a workhouse, and the needlework 'falling off bit by bit,' this girl suffered, for nine months, every extremity of dire distress. Being one night without any food or shelter from the weather, she went to the lodging of a woman who had once lived in the same house with herself and her mother, and asked to be allowed to lie down on the stairs. She was refused, and stole a shawl which she sold for a penny. A fortnight afterwards, being still in a starving and houseless state, she went back to the same woman's, and preferred the same request. Again refused, she stole a bible from her, which she sold for twopence. The theft was immediately discovered, and she was taken as she lay asleep in the casual ward of a workhouse. These facts were distinctly proved upon her trial. She was sentenced to three months' imprisonment, and was then admitted into the Home. She has never been corrupted. She remained in the Home, bearing an excellent character, a little more than a year; emigrated; conducted herself uniformly well in a good situation; and is now married.

Case number forty-one was a pretty girl of a quiet and good manner, aged nineteen. She came from a watering-place where she had lived with her mother until within a couple of years, when her mother married again and she was considered an incumbrance at a very bad home. She became apprenticed to a dressmaker, who, on account of staying out beyond the prescribed hours one night when she went with some other young people to a Circus, positively refused to admit her or give her any shelter from the streets. The natural consequences of this unjustifiable behaviour followed. She came to the Home on the recommendation of a clergyman to whom she fortunately applied, when in a state of sickness and misery too deplorable to be even suggested to the reader's imagination. She remained in the Home (with an interval of hospital treatment) upwards of a year and a half, when she was sent abroad. Her character is irreproachable, and she is industrious, happy and full of gratitude.

Case number fifty was a very homely, clumsy, ignorant girl, supposed to be about nineteen, but who again had no knowledge of her birthday. She was taken from a Ragged School; her mother had died when she was a little girl; and her father, marrying again, had turned her out of doors, though her mother-in-law had been kind to her. She had been once in prison for breaking some windows near the Mansion House, 'having nowheres as you can think of, to go to.' She had never gone wrong otherwise, and particularly wished that 'to be wrote down.' She was in as dirty and unwholesome a condition, on her admission, as she could well be, but was inconsolable at the idea of losing her hair, until the fortunate suggestion was made that it would grow more luxuriantly after shaving. She then consented, with many tears, to that (in her case) indispensable operation. This deserted and unfortunate creature, after a short period of depression began to brighten, uniformly showed a very honest and truthful nature, and after remaining in the Home a year, has recently emigrated; a thoroughly good plain servant, with every susceptibility for forming a faithful and affectionate attachment to her employers.

Case number fifty-eight was a girl of nineteen, all but starved through inability to live by needlework. She had never gone wrong, was gradually brought into a good bodily condition, invariably conducted herself well, and went abroad, rescued and happy.

Case number fifty-one was a little ragged girl of sixteen or seventeen, as she said; but of very juvenile appearance. She was put to the bar at a Police Office, with two much older women, regular vagrants, for making a disturbance at the workhouse gate on the previous night on being refused relief. She had been a professed tramp for six or seven years, knew of no relation, and had had no friends but one old woman, whose very name she did not appear to be sure of. Her father, a scaffold builder, she had 'lost' on London Bridge when she was ten or eleven years old. There appeared little doubt that he had purposely abandoned her, but she had no suspicion of it. She had long been hop-picking in the hop season, and wandering about the country at all seasons, and was unaccustomed to shoes, and had seldom slept in a bed. She answered some searching questions without the least reserve, and not at all in her own favour. Her appearance of destitution was in perfect keeping with her story. This girl was received into the Home. Within a year, there was clinging round the principal Superintendent's neck, on board a ship bound for Australia – in a state of grief at parting that moved the bystanders to tears – a pretty little neat modest useful girl, against whom not a moment's complaint had been made, and who had diligently learnt everything that had been set before her.

Case number fifty-four, a good-looking young woman of two-and-twenty, was first seen in prison under remand on a charge of attempting to commit suicide. Her mother had died before she was two years old, and her father had married again; but she spoke in high and affectionate terms both of her father and her mother-in-law. She had been a travelling maid with an elderly lady, and, on her mistress going to Russia, had returned home to her father's. She had stayed out late one night, in company with a 'commissioner' whom she had known abroad, was afraid or ashamed to go home, and so went wrong. Falling lower, and becoming poorer, she became at last acquainted with a ticket-taker at a railway station, who tired of the acquaintance. One night when he had made an appointment (as he had often done before) and, on the plea of inability to leave his duties, had put this girl in a cab, that she might be taken safely home (she seemed to have inspired him with that much enduring regard), she pulled up the window and swallowed two shillings' worth of the essential oil of almonds which she had bought at a chemist's an hour before. The driver happened to look round when she still had the bottle to her lips, immediately made out the whole story, and had the presence of mind to drive her straight to a hospital, where she remained a month before she was cured. She was in that state of depression in the prison, that it was a matter for grave consideration whether it would be safe to take her into the Home, where, if she were bent upon committing suicide, it would be almost impossible to prevent her. After some talk with her, however, it was decided to receive her. She proved one of the best inmates it has ever had, and remained in it seven months before she emigrated. Her father, who had never seen her since the night of her staying out late, came to see her in the Home, and confirmed these particulars. It is doubtful whether any treatment but that pursued in such an institution would have restored this girl.

Case number fourteen was an extremely pretty girl of twenty, whose mother was married to a second husband – a drunken man who ill-treated his step-daughter. She had been engaged to be married, but had been deceived, and had run away from home in shame, and had been away three years. Within that period, however, she had twice returned home; the first time for six months; the second time for a few days. She had also been in a London hospital. She had also been in the Magdalen:[33] which institution her father-in-law, with a drunkard's inconsistency, had induced her to leave, to attend her mother's funeral – and then ill-treated her as before. She had been once in prison as a disorderly character, and was received from the prison into the Home. Her health was impaired and her experiences had been of a bad kind in a bad quarter of London, but she was still a girl of remarkably engaging and delicate appearance. She remained in the Home, improving rapidly, thirteen months. She was never complained of, and her general deportment was unusually quiet and modest. She emigrated, and is a good, industrious, happy wife.

This paper can scarcely be better closed than by the following pretty passage from a letter of one of the married young women.

HONNOURED LADIES,

I have again taken the liberty of writing to you to let you know how I am going on since I last wrote Home for I can never forget that name that still comes fresh to my mind, Honnoured Ladies I received your most kind letter on Tuesday the 21st of May my Mistress was kind enough to bring it over to me she told me that she also had a letter from you and that she should write Home and give you a good account of us. Honnoured Ladies I cannot describe the feelings which I felt on receiving your most kind letter, I first read my letter then I cried but it was with tears of joy, to think you was so kind to write to us Honnoured Ladies I have seen Jane and I showed my letter and she is going write Home, she is living about 36 miles from where I live and her and her husband are very happy together she has been down to our Town this week and it is the first that we have seen of her since a week after they were married. My Husband is very kind to me and we live very happy and comfortable together we have a nice garden where we grow all that we want we have sown some peas turnips and I helped to do some we have three such nice pigs and we killed one last week he was so fat that he could not see out of his eyes he used to have to sit down to eat and I have got such a nice cat – she peeps over me while I am writing this. My Husband was going out one day, and he heard that cat cry and he fetched her in she was so thin. My tow little birds are gone – one dide and the other flew away now I have got none, get down Cat do. My Husband has built a shed at the side of the house to do any thing for hisself when he coms home from work of a night he tells me that I shall every 9 years com Home if we live so long please

> God, but I think that he is only making game of me. Honnoured Ladies I can never feel grateful enough for your kindness to me and the kind indulgences which I received at my happy Home, I often wish that I could come Home and see that happy place again once more and all my kind friends which I hope I may one day please God.

No comments or arguments shall be added to swell the length this account has already attained. Our readers will judge for themselves what some of these cases must have soon become, but for the timely interposition of the Home established by the Ladies whose charity is so discreet and so impartial.

A December Vision

I saw a mighty Spirit, traversing the world without any rest or pause. It was omnipresent, it was all-powerful, it had no compunction, no pity, no relenting sense that any appeal from any of the race of men could reach. It was invisible to every creature born upon the earth, save once to each. It turned its shaded face on whatsoever living thing, one time; and straight the end of that thing was come. It passed through the forest, and the vigorous tree it looked on shrunk away; through the garden, and the leaves perished and the flowers withered; through the air, and the eagles flagged upon the wing and dropped; through the sea, and the monsters of the deep floated, great wrecks, upon the waters. It met the eyes of lions in their lairs, and they were dust; its shadow darkened the faces of young children lying asleep, and they awoke no more.

It had its work appointed it; it inexorably did what was appointed to it to do; and neither sped nor slackened. Called to, it went on unmoved, and did not come. Besought, by some who felt that it was drawing near, to change its course, it turned its shaded face upon them, even while they cried, and they were dumb. It passed into the midst of palace chambers, where there were lights and music, pictures, diamonds, gold and silver; crossed the wrinkled and the grey, regardless of them; looked into the eyes of a bright bride; and vanished. It revealed itself to the baby on the old crone's knee, and left the old crone wailing by the fire. But, whether the beholder of its face were, now a King, or now a labourer, now a Queen, or now a seamstress; let the hand it palsied, be on the sceptre, or the plough, or yet too small and nerveless to grasp anything: the Spirit never paused in its appointed work, and, sooner or later, turned its impartial face on all.

I saw a Minister of State, sitting in his Closet; and, round about him, rising from the country which he governed, up to the Eternal Heavens, was a low dull howl of Ignorance. It was a wild, inexplicable mutter, confused, but full of threatening, and it made all hearers' hearts to quake within them. But, few heard. In the single city where this Minister of State was seated, I saw Thirty Thousand children, hunted, flogged, imprisoned, but not taught – who might have been nurtured by the wolf or bear, so little of humanity had they, within them or without – all joining in this doleful cry. And, ever among them, as among all ranks and grades of mortals, in all parts of the globe, the Spirit went; and ever by thousands, in their brutish state, with all the gifts of God perverted in their breasts or trampled out, they died.

The Minister of State, whose heart was pierced by even the little he could hear of these terrible voices, day and night rising to Heaven, went among the Priests and Teachers of all denominations, and faintly said:

'Hearken to this dreadful cry! What shall we do to stay it?'

One body of respondents answered, 'Teach this!'

Another said, 'Teach that!'

Another said, 'Teach neither this nor that, but t'other!'

Another quarrelled with all the three; twenty others quarrelled with all the four, and quarrelled no less bitterly among themselves. The voices, not stayed by this, cried out day and night; and still, among those many thousands, as among all mankind, went the Spirit, who never rested from its labour; and still, in brutish sort, they died.

Then, a whisper murmured to the Minister of State:

'Correct this for thyself. Be bold! Silence these voices, or virtuously lose thy power in the attempt to do it. Thou cans't not sow a grain of good seed in vain. Thou knowest it well. Be bold, and do thy duty!'

The Minister shrugged his shoulders, and replied, 'It is a great wrong – BUT IT WILL LAST MY TIME.' And so he put it from him.

Then, the whisper went among the Priests and Teachers, saying to each, 'In thy soul thou knowest it is a truth, O, man, that there are good things to be taught, on which all men may agree. Teach those, and stay this cry.'

To which, each answered in like manner, 'It is a great wrong – BUT IT WILL LAST MY TIME.' And so *he* put it from him.

I saw a poisoned air, in which Life drooped. I saw Disease, arrayed in all its store of hideous aspects and appalling shapes, triumphant in every alley, bye-way, court, back-street, and poor abode, in every place where human beings congregated – in the proudest and most boastful places, most of all. I saw innumerable hosts, fore-doomed to darkness, dirt, pestilence obscenity, misery, and early death. I saw, wheresoever I looked, cunning preparations made for defacing the Creator's Image, from the moment of its appearance here on earth, and stamping over it the image of the Devil. I saw, from those reeking and pernicious stews, the avenging consequences of such Sin issuing forth, and penetrating to the highest places. I saw the rich struck down in their strength, their darling children weakened and withered, their marriageable sons and daughters perish in their prime. I saw that not one miserable wretch breathed out his poisoned life in the deepest cellar of the most neglected town, but, from the surrounding atmosphere, some particles of his infection were borne away, charged with heavy retribution on the general guilt.

There were many attentive and alarmed persons looking on, who saw these things too. They were well clothed, and had purses in their pockets; they were educated, full of kindness, and loved mercy. They said to one another, 'This is horrible, and shall not be!' and there was a stir among them to set it right. But, opposed to these, came a small multitude of noisy fools and greedy knaves, whose harvest was in such horrors; and they, with impudence and turmoil, and with scurrilous jests at misery and death, repelled the better lookers-on, who soon fell back, and stood aloof.

There, the whisper went among those better lookers-on, saying, 'Over the bodies of those fellows, to the remedy!'

But, each of them moodily shrugged his shoulders, and replied, 'It is a great wrong – BUT IT WILL LAST MY TIME!' And so they put it from them.

I saw a great library of laws and law-proceedings, so complicated, costly, and unintelligible, that, although numbers of lawyers united in a public fiction that these were wonderfully just and equal, there was scarcely an honest man among them, but who said to his friend, privately consulting him, 'Better put up with a fraud or other injury than grope for redress through the manifold blind turnings and strange chances of this system.'

I saw a portion of the system, called (of all things) EQUITY,[34] which was ruin to suitors, ruin to property, a shield for wrong-doers having money, a rack for right-doers having none; a by-word for delay, slow agony of mind, despair, impoverishment, trickery, confusion, insupportable injustice. A main part of it, I saw prisoners wasting in jail; mad people babbling in hospitals; suicides chronicled in the yearly records; orphans robbed of their inheritance; infants righted (perhaps) when they were grey.

Certain lawyers and laymen came together, and said to one another, 'In only one of these our Courts of Equity, there are years of this dark perspective before us at the present moment. We must change this.'

'Uprose, immediately, a throng of others, Secretaries, Petty Bags, Hanapers, Chaff-waxes, and what not, singing (in answer) 'Rule Britannia,' and 'God save the Queen;' making flourishing speeches, pronouncing hard names, demanding committees, commissions, commissioners, and other scarecrows, and terrifying the little band of innovators out of their five wits.

Then, the whisper went among the latter, as they shrunk back, saying, 'If there is any wrong within the universal knowledge, this wrong is. Go on! Set it right!'

Whereon, each of them sorrowfully thrust his hands in his pockets, and replied, 'It is indeed a great wrong; – BUT IT WILL LAST MY TIME!' – and so *they* put it from them.

The Spirit with its face concealed, summoned all the people who had used this phrase about their Time, into its presence. Then, it said, beginning with the Minister of State: 'Of what duration is *your* Time?'

The Minister of State replied, 'My ancient family has always been long-lived. My father died at eighty-four; my grandfather, at ninety-two. We have the gout, but bear it (like our honours) many years.'

'And you,' said the Spirit to the Priests and Teachers, 'what may *your* time be?'

Some, believed that they were so strong, as that they should number many more years than threescore and ten; others, were the sons of old incumbents who had long outlived youthful expectants. Others, for any means they had of calculating, might be long-lived or short-lived – generally (they had a strong persuasion) long. So, among the well-clothed lookers-on. So, among the lawyers and laymen.

'But, every man, as I understand you, one and all,' said the Spirit, 'has his time?'

'Yes!' they exclaimed together.

'Yes,' said the Spirit; 'and it is – ETERNITY! Whosoever is a consenting party to a wrong, comforting himself with the base reflection that it will last his time, shall bear his portion of that wrong throughout ALL TIME. And, in that hour when he and I stand face to face, he shall surely know it, as my name is Death!'

It departed, turning its shaded face hither and thither as it passed along upon its ceaseless work, and blighting all on whom it looked.

Then went among many trembling hearers the whisper, saying, 'See, each of you, before you take your ease, O wicked, selfish men, that what will 'last your time,' be just enough to last for ever!'

Notes

1. The Rev. Sydney Smith (1771–1845) was an essayist who made regular contributions to the Victorian press.
2. The titular hero of Voltaire's *Candide* (1758) is optimistic to the point of naivety; he begins his story in the country home of Baron Thunder-ten Tronckh, which to Candide's innocent eyes is a mansion.
3. Thomas Wakley (1795–1862) was a controversial reformer; he is referenced also in George Eliot's *Middlemarch*, and won the respect of Dickens after he sat on a jury during a trial conducted by Wakley, which Dickens referred to in a later article, 'Some Recollections of Mortality' (part of the *Uncommercial Traveller* series, printed in *All the Year Round*, 16 May 1863).
4. *Participes criminis* translates as partners-in-crime.
5. In April 1840, there was a peaceful procession in London by Chartists to present a petition, which sparked fears of a revolution and led to an increased presence of officers; later that year in August there was a Chartist uprising and several ringleaders were arrested to foil the plot.
6. George Catlin (1796–1872) first presented his exhibition at the Egyptian Hall in London in 1840, in which Native American artefacts and paintings were on show; the show continued for many years and in other locations as well, with Catlin bringing in Native American performers to encourage more visitors.
7. The Ojibbeway (or Ojibway) are a tribe of Native Americans, such as would have been seen in Catlin's exhibit, and later recorded in his work *The Adventures of the Ojibbeway and Ioway Indians* (1852).
8. Noodledom, as the name suggests, is the world of fools; Dickens refers to it again in *Bleak House*.
9. George W. M. Reynolds (1814–1879) was a best-selling author of the time who has since fallen into obscurity; he held Chartist views, as did his friend and reformer Charles Cochrane, and it is safe to assume that the talks to which Dickens refers here would have been to that effect.
10. James Ferguson (1799–1880) was a self-taught watchmaker who went on to become one of the best in England.
11. For ankecher, read handkerchief.
12. This refers to Walter Scott's *Letters on Demonology and Witchcraft* (1830), a collection of fictional letters, of which the first one makes reference to a spirit in the form of 'a gentleman-usher, dressed as if to wait upon a Lord Lieutenant of Ireland, a Lord High Commissioner of the Kirk, or any other who bears on his brow the rank and stamp of delegated sovereignty' who, along with other apparitions, haunts a man.

13. An Itch ward is the nineteenth-century equivalent of an STD clinic; such a woman as might be found there was immortalised by William Hogarth (1697–1764) in his series of pictures *The Harlot's Progress*.
14. For sodgers, read soldiers.
15. Newgate Prison features throughout Dickens' works, in *Oliver Twist*, *A Tale of Two Cities*, *Barnaby Rudge* and more centrally in 'A Visit to Newgate' in *Sketches by Boz*.
16. A porringer is a small dish that was generally used for serving gruel or porridge; its use here to serve a Sunday roast is an ironic commentary on the portions.
17. In the previous report by Dickens as the Uncommercial Traveller, 'Shy Neighbourhoods' (published in *All the Year Round* on 26 May 1860), he discusses his tendencies to wander around like a 'vagabond' and states 'I think I must be the descendant, at no great distance, of some irreclaimable tramp.'
18. Pow is another term for head.
19. *Fruges consumere nati* is a phrase attributed to Horace, its literal meaning being 'those born to consume the fruits of the earth', but its implication here being a patronising reference to the uneducated masses.
20. The Crispin and Crispanus is a pub near Gadshill.
21. A Cheap Jack was a pedlar or travelling merchant, here and in the rest of the passage Dickens draws upon stock types as seen in travelling entertainment as he describes the show-tramps he sees.
22. Norfolk Island was a penal colony in New South Wales with a reputation for 'the worst description of convicts', in the words of its governor Thomas Brisbane in 1824.
23. According to Peter Cunningham's *Handbook of London* (1850), the Mendicity Society 'gives meals and money, supplies mill and other work to applicants, investigates begging-letter cases, and apprehends vagrants and impostors.'
24. Smith wrote a letter dated 3 November 1843 to the *Morning Chronicle* (in which Dickens himself had published articles), in which the quotation of 'the dangerous luxury of dishonesty' is mentioned in relation to a dispute Smith had with the state of Pennsylvania after he lent money for general improvements, and the loan was not repaid.
25. Tippoo (or Tipu) Sahib was Sultan of India from 1782–1799 and a staunch opponent of the East India Trading Company who captured the imagination of several artists and writers in Britain. In contrast, the writer Charles Lamb (1775–1834) worked at the India house from 1792 to 1817.
26. Dickens is dropping references to past works here: the little midshipman adorns the shop of Walter Gay and his uncle Sol Gills in *Dombey and Son*, while the Saracen's Head is the coaching inn at which Mr Squeers resides

while in London and from which Nicholas Nickleby departs for Squeer's school in Yorkshire.

27. In the song 'Wapping Old Stairs', the heroine Molly berates her lover Tom for doubting her constancy and makes reference to a tobacco box she gave him with her name on it.

28. Mrs Gamp from *Martin Chuzzlewit* was one of Dickens' most popular characters in his lifetime; she acted as a midwife and nurse to the ill, though her level of care was debatable; though *Chuzzlewit* was written in 1843–4, at the time of writing this article, Dickens was in the midst of his public readings, one of which was 'Mrs Gamp', so the character was still contemporary to the article.

29. A refractory was a place in the workhouse used as a punishment for the inmates, where they would be kept separate from the others in the workhouse – a sort of group solitary confinement.

30. This book, since lost, is of great interest to Dickens scholars, as they contain notes from Dickens' interviews with the ladies of Urania cottage, and are believed to have provided the inspiration for several of Dickens' female characters (and can be considered to have provided much of the material for this article also).

31. Captain Alexander Maconochie was, for a time, governor of Norfolk Island (see note 22) where he promoted ideas controversial for the time, later made more public through his book *Crime and Punishment* (1846), in which he advocated reward as well as punishment, and indeed attacked most forms of punishment as purely vindictive rather than corrective. Dickens owned Maconochie's book, and the pair met to discuss his ideas.

32. The meaning of temperance hinted at by Dickens here is its use by Temperance Societies who advocated complete abstinence from alcohol.

33. The Magdalen Hospital, founded in the mid-eighteenth century, was known for its work helping penitent prostitutes.

34. The courts of equity, or chancery courts, were most extensively ripped apart by Dickens in *Bleak House* a year after this article was written, where the case of Jarndyce vs. Jarndyce has been drawn out for several years and made misery and financial woe for the claimants.

Biographical note

Charles Dickens (1812–70), a true celebrity in the Victorian period, remains one of the best-known British writers. His most popular works, such as *Great Expectations* (1861) and *A Christmas Carol* (1843), continue to be read and adapted worldwide. In addition to fourteen complete novels, Dickens wrote short stories, essays, and plays.

At the age of ten, Dickens moved with his family from Chatham to London. Though his travels would later take him abroad, most notably to America, his permanent home remained in the city for the duration of his life. His early life was financially and emotionally unstable, and when his father was imprisoned for debt, he was sent to work in a blacking factory, an experience that haunted his later fiction. He worked as an office-boy and court reporter before his *Sketches by Boz* (1836–7) brought his writing to the attention of the publishing house Chapman and Hall. After the success of *The Posthumous Papers of the Pickwick Club*, Dickens was able to found the journal *Bentley's Miscellany*, and from then on all his major novels were published as serial instalments in his own magazines.

After more than twenty years of marriage, in 1858, Dickens abruptly separated from his wife Catherine, mother of his ten children, in order to pursue a relationship with Ellen Ternan, a young actress. He died suddenly in 1870, leaving his novel, *The Mystery of Edwin Drood*, unfinished.

Pete Orford is a research fellow at the University of Buckingham, where he is currently researching the seemingly endless number of solutions and sequels to Dickens' last work, *The Mystery of Edwin Drood*. He has written several articles and conference papers on Dickens, not to mention editing the previous collections of Dickens' writings for Hesperus Press: *On Travel*, *On London* and *On Theatre*. Away from Dickens, he has written groundbreaking articles on Fitz-James O'Brien, and edited a collection of his stories, *The Diamond Lens and Other Stories*, also for Hesperus Press.

HESPERUS PRESS

Hesperus Press is committed to bringing near what is far – far both in space and time. Works written by the greatest authors, and unjustly neglected or simply little known in the English-speaking world, are made accessible through new translations and a completely fresh editorial approach. Through these classic works, the reader is introduced to the greatest writers from all times and all cultures.

For more information on Hesperus Press, please visit our website: **www.hesperuspress.com**

SELECTED TITLES FROM HESPERUS PRESS

Author	*Title*	*Foreword writer*
Pietro Aretino	*The School of Whoredom*	Paul Bailey
Pietro Aretino	*The Secret Life of Nuns*	
Jane Austen	*Lesley Castle*	Zoë Heller
Jane Austen	*Love and Friendship*	Fay Weldon
Honoré de Balzac	*Colonel Chabert*	A.N. Wilson
Charles Baudelaire	*On Wine and Hashish*	Margaret Drabble
Giovanni Boccaccio	*Life of Dante*	A.N. Wilson
Charlotte Brontë	*The Spell*	
Emily Brontë	*Poems of Solitude*	Helen Dunmore
Mikhail Bulgakov	*Fatal Eggs*	Doris Lessing
Mikhail Bulgakov	*The Heart of a Dog*	A.S. Byatt
Giacomo Casanova	*The Duel*	Tim Parks
Miguel de Cervantes	*The Dialogue of the Dogs*	Ben Okri
Geoffrey Chaucer	*The Parliament of Birds*	
Anton Chekhov	*The Story of a Nobody*	Louis de Bernières
Anton Chekhov	*Three Years*	William Fiennes
Wilkie Collins	*The Frozen Deep*	
Joseph Conrad	*Heart of Darkness*	A.N. Wilson
Joseph Conrad	*The Return*	Colm Tóibín
Gabriele D'Annunzio	*The Book of the Virgins*	Tim Parks
Dante Alighieri	*The Divine Comedy: Inferno*	
Dante Alighieri	*New Life*	Louis de Bernières
Daniel Defoe	*The King of Pirates*	Peter Ackroyd
Marquis de Sade	*Incest*	Janet Street-Porter
Charles Dickens	*The Haunted House*	Peter Ackroyd
Charles Dickens	*A House to Let*	
Fyodor Dostoevsky	*The Double*	Jeremy Dyson
Fyodor Dostoevsky	*Poor People*	Charlotte Hobson
Alexandre Dumas	*One Thousand and One Ghosts*	

George Eliot	*Amos Barton*	Matthew Sweet
Henry Fielding	*Jonathan Wild the Great*	Peter Ackroyd
F. Scott Fitzgerald	*The Popular Girl*	Helen Dunmore
Gustave Flaubert	*Memoirs of a Madman*	Germaine Greer
Ugo Foscolo	*Last Letters of Jacopo Ortis*	Valerio Massimo Manfredi
Elizabeth Gaskell	*Lois the Witch*	Jenny Uglow
Théophile Gautier	*The Jinx*	Gilbert Adair
André Gide	*Theseus*	
Johann Wolfgang von Goethe	*The Man of Fifty*	A.S. Byatt
Nikolai Gogol	*The Squabble*	Patrick McCabe
E.T.A. Hoffmann	*Mademoiselle de Scudéri*	Gilbert Adair
Victor Hugo	*The Last Day of a Condemned Man*	Libby Purves
Joris-Karl Huysmans	*With the Flow*	Simon Callow
Henry James	*In the Cage*	Libby Purves
Franz Kafka	*Metamorphosis*	Martin Jarvis
Franz Kafka	*The Trial*	Zadie Smith
John Keats	*Fugitive Poems*	Andrew Motion
Heinrich von Kleist	*The Marquise of O–*	Andrew Miller
Mikhail Lermontov	*A Hero of Our Time*	Doris Lessing
Nikolai Leskov	*Lady Macbeth of Mtsensk*	Gilbert Adair
Carlo Levi	*Words are Stones*	Anita Desai
Xavier de Maistre	*A Journey Around my Room*	Alain de Botton
André Malraux	*The Way of the Kings*	Rachel Seiffert
Katherine Mansfield	*Prelude*	William Boyd
Edgar Lee Masters	*Spoon River Anthology*	Shena Mackay
Guy de Maupassant	*Butterball*	Germaine Greer
Prosper Mérimée	*Carmen*	Philip Pullman
Sir Thomas More	*The History of King Richard III*	Sister Wendy Beckett
Sándor Petőfi	*John the Valiant*	George Szirtes

Francis Petrarch	*My Secret Book*	Germaine Greer
Luigi Pirandello	*Loveless Love*	
Edgar Allan Poe	*Eureka*	Sir Patrick Moore
Alexander Pope	*The Rape of the Lock* and *A Key to the Lock*	Peter Ackroyd
Antoine-François Prévost	*Manon Lescaut*	Germaine Greer
Marcel Proust	*Pleasures and Days*	A.N. Wilson
Alexander Pushkin	*Dubrovsky*	Patrick Neate
Alexander Pushkin	*Ruslan and Lyudmila*	Colm Tóibín
François Rabelais	*Pantagruel*	Paul Bailey
François Rabelais	*Gargantua*	Paul Bailey
Christina Rossetti	*Commonplace*	Andrew Motion
George Sand	*The Devil's Pool*	Victoria Glendinning
Jean-Paul Sartre	*The Wall*	Justin Cartwright
Friedrich von Schiller	*The Ghost-seer*	Martin Jarvis
Mary Shelley	*Transformation*	
Percy Bysshe Shelley	*Zastrozzi*	Germaine Greer
Stendhal	*Memoirs of an Egotist*	Doris Lessing
Stendhal	*On Love*	A.C. Grayling
Robert Louis Stevenson	*Dr Jekyll and Mr Hyde*	Helen Dunmore
Theodor Storm	*The Lake of the Bees*	Alan Sillitoe
Leo Tolstoy	*The Death of Ivan Ilych*	
Leo Tolstoy	*Hadji Murat*	Colm Tóibín
Ivan Turgenev	*Faust*	Simon Callow
Mark Twain	*The Diary of Adam and Eve*	John Updike
Mark Twain	*Tom Sawyer, Detective*	
Oscar Wilde	*The Portrait of Mr W.H.*	Peter Ackroyd
Virginia Woolf	*Carlyle's House and Other Sketches*	Doris Lessing
Virginia Woolf	*Monday or Tuesday*	Scarlett Thomas
Emile Zola	*For a Night of Love*	A.N. Wilson